Sins of the Internet

Escaping the Psychological Traps of the Digital Age

Richard Lowe

The Writing King

Sins of the Internet: Escaping the Psychological Traps of the Digital Age

Table of Contents

See books by Richard Lowe at

https://masterofworlds.com

Get free publishing insights and industry updates at

https://thewritingking.substack.com

For ghostwriting and book coaching services see

https://thewritingking.com

Introduction: The Digital Fall from Grace

Remember when the internet was going to save us all? Remember when we thought this magical network would democratize information, connect humanity, and usher in an age of enlightenment? What a joke.

We were promised a digital utopia. We got a surveillance nightmare wrapped in colorful apps and addictive notifications. The internet would make us smarter, more connected, more empathetic. Instead, it made us angrier, more isolated, and more gullible than any generation before us.

The internet didn't democratize information. It weaponized it. It didn't connect us. It divided us into warring tribes of keyboard warriors. It didn't enlighten us. It made us easier to fool with fake news, conspiracy theories, and digital snake oil.

Every promise they made got perverted into its opposite. The World Wide Web became the World Wide Trap. Social media became antisocial media. The information superhighway became the misinformation superhighway. We're all stuck in traffic, honking our horns at each other while tech billionaires count their money.

The worst part? We did this to ourselves. We handed over our attention, our data, our relationships, and our mental health to companies whose entire business model depends on making us miserable. We became the product being sold, and we paid for the privilege.

This book isn't about technical failures. Plenty of smart people have written about algorithms and data breaches and privacy violations. This is about moral failures. This is about how we took the most powerful communication tool in human history and turned it into a machine for generating outrage, addiction, and despair.

We're living through the digital equivalent of the fall from Eden, except we ate the apple knowing full well it was poisoned. We saw the warning signs. Facebook was making us depressed.

Twitter was making us angry. TikTok was rotting our brains. We kept using them anyway.

The internet has committed every sin in the book, then invented a few new ones. It made us wrathful with endless outrage cycles. It made us greedy for likes and follows and digital validation. It made us envious of everyone else's carefully curated highlight reels. It made us prideful in our echo chambers where we're always right and everyone else is always wrong.

The internet also made us lustful for artificial intimacy with strangers. It made us gluttonous for information we can't digest. It made us slothful in our thinking, letting algorithms decide what we see and believe. Beyond the classical sins, it created entirely new forms of moral corruption that would make medieval theologians weep.

We're drowning in deception. Deepfakes and misinformation campaigns flood our feeds. We're suffocating under the weight of our own vanity, performing our lives for an audience of strangers. We're tearing each other apart with digital tribalism that makes ancient blood feuds look civilized. We're forgetting everything while remembering every stupid thing everyone ever said online.

We've become apathetic to real suffering while getting worked up over manufactured controversies. We're addicted to digital stimulation like lab rats pressing a lever for cocaine. We've turned human relationships into content to be monetized, packaged, and sold to the highest bidder.

This isn't progress. This is regression. We took the most powerful tool for human connection ever created and used it to make ourselves more disconnected than ever. We took the greatest repository of human knowledge and filled it with garbage. We took the ultimate platform for free expression and turned it into a censorship playground where mobs decide who gets to speak.

The tech companies will tell you this is just growing pains. They're working on solutions. The next update, the next feature, the next platform will fix everything. They're lying. They have no incentive to fix anything because broken is profitable. Outraged users are engaged users. Addicted users are loyal users. Miserable users are profitable users.

Here's what makes me furious: we don't have to live like this. None of this was inevitable. Every single one of these problems was a choice. Someone decided to build addiction into these platforms. Someone decided to amplify anger over empathy. Someone decided to prioritize engagement over wellbeing. Someone decided to treat human attention like a resource to be strip-mined.

We can make different choices. We can demand better. We can build better. We can use these tools without letting them use us. First, we need to acknowledge how far we've fallen. We need to catalog the sins, confess our complicity, and commit to something better.

The internet promised to make us more human. Instead, it's making us less human every day. Time to take our humanity back. We can't do that until we understand exactly what we've lost and how we lost it.

Welcome to the confessional. Time to face our digital sins.

Chapter 1: Wrath - The Rage Machine

The internet was supposed to give everyone a voice. Instead, it gave everyone a megaphone to scream at each other.

Here's what really happened: tech companies discovered that angry people click more. They click faster, stay longer, and share more content. Anger became the internet's jet fuel, and every platform started optimizing for maximum fury.

Facebook's own internal research proved this. In 2018, their data scientists found that posts generating angry reactions got six times more engagement than posts generating happy reactions. Did they fix this? No. They doubled down. The algorithm started serving users more content designed to piss them off because pissed-off users are profitable users.

Twitter took this logic even further. They built a platform around hot takes and gotcha moments. The 280-character limit forces nuance out of every conversation. Complex ideas get compressed into bumper stickers. Thoughtful responses get buried under waves of snark and outrage. The platform literally rewards the worst possible version of every argument.

YouTube figured out that controversy keeps people watching. Their recommendation algorithm pushes users toward increasingly extreme content because extreme content generates longer viewing sessions. Start with a cooking video, end up watching conspiracy theories about how the government is poisoning your food. The algorithm doesn't care about truth. It cares about watch time.

The result? We live in a constant state of manufactured outrage. Every day brings a new main character for the internet to destroy. Some college student says something stupid, and within hours, thousands of strangers are competing to ruin their life. A comedian makes a bad joke, and the digital mob demands their career be ended. A restaurant gets a bad review, and the pile-on turns into a harassment campaign.

This isn't justice. It's digital blood sport.

Take the Justine Sacco case. A PR executive made a thoughtless joke about AIDS in Africa before boarding a plane. By the time she landed eleven hours later, she'd become the top trending topic worldwide. Tens of thousands of people had called for her to be fired, doxxed, and worse. Her employer fired her before she even knew what was happening.

Was the joke offensive? Sure. Did it deserve to destroy someone's entire life? The internet mob thought so. They felt righteous doing it. They were fighting racism, they told themselves. They were making the world better by destroying one woman's career over a single tweet.

But here's the thing: none of those people actually cared about AIDS in Africa. They cared about the rush of participating in a digital lynching. They got to feel morally superior while engaging in the most toxic behavior imaginable. The platforms made money from every angry click, every outraged share, every self-righteous comment.

The Boston Marathon bombing showed us where this logic leads. Reddit users decided they could solve the case better than the FBI. They formed digital posses to hunt down the bombers using grainy photos and wild speculation. They falsely accused multiple innocent people, including a missing student whose family was already dealing with tragedy. The mob was so convinced of their righteousness that facts became irrelevant.

This pattern repeats constantly now. Someone gets accused of something online, and the digital mob bypasses due process entirely. They become judge, jury, and executioner based on screenshots and hearsay. The platforms profit from the chaos while the accused person's life gets destroyed in real time.

The platforms know exactly what they're doing. Internal Facebook documents leaked in 2021 showed that company researchers had repeatedly warned executives that their algorithms were promoting divisive content and harming users' mental health. The executives' response? Keep the engagement-driven algorithms running because changing them would hurt profits.

YouTube's recommendation engine has arguably radicalized more people than any extremist organization in history. It starts innocently enough. Someone searches for workout videos and gets recommended fitness content. But the algorithm gradually pushes toward more extreme content because extreme content generates more engagement. Before long, that person is watching videos about how vaccines are poison and the government is trying to control their mind.

The algorithm doesn't have a political agenda. It has a profit agenda. It will push you toward whatever keeps you watching, whether that's flat earth theories, QAnon conspiracies, or radical political content. Your uncle didn't become a conspiracy theorist by accident. YouTube's recommendation engine guided him there one video at a time.

Dating apps have weaponized rejection. Getting turned down used to be a private embarrassment. Now it becomes a public harassment campaign. Screenshots of dating conversations go viral with the rejected person's face and personal information attached. Entire subreddits exist to shame people for their dating profiles. We've turned human connection into content for the outrage machine.

Even innocent hobby communities get infected. Knitting forums split into warring factions over social justice issues. Cooking groups become battlegrounds for political arguments. Board game communities tear themselves apart over representation and inclusivity. The rage machine consumes everything because anger travels faster than any other emotion online.

Politicians figured out the game early. Why build coalitions when you can build fundraising campaigns around outrage? Why compromise when controversy generates more donations and media coverage? Political discourse became performance art designed to generate viral moments and angry small-dollar donations.

The media adapted too. Reasonable analysis doesn't drive traffic. Measured takes don't trend. But tell people their way of life is under attack, that their enemies are plotting against them, that everything they value is being destroyed, and watch those engagement numbers explode.

Social media influencers built entire careers on manufactured controversy. They don't say outrageous things because they believe them. They say outrageous things because outrage is their business model. They're human clickbait, professional pot-stirrers whose job is generating the anger that keeps the machine running.

We're raising children in this environment. They're learning that the proper response to disagreement is total warfare. They're being trained to see enemies everywhere and respond to conflict with maximum aggression. We're creating a generation that doesn't know how to have civil conversations about difficult topics.

The rage machine has a body count. Teen suicide rates spiked alongside social media adoption. Online harassment campaigns have driven people to self-harm and worse. The constant state of outrage is destroying our mental health, our relationships, and our ability to function as a society.

But here's what makes this truly infuriating: it's all deliberate. Every design choice, every algorithm tweak, every platform feature is optimized to generate maximum engagement through maximum outrage. The tech companies have turned human anger into their most valuable product, and they're getting rich selling our fury back to us.

The internet promised to connect us. Instead, it turned us into an army of angry strangers ready to destroy each other over the smallest disagreements. The rage machine is working exactly as designed. The only question is whether we're going to keep feeding it or finally pull the plug.

What Do You Do About This?

The first move is the hardest: stop dunking. Every time you share an outrage post, write an angry comment, or join a pile-on, you're doing the platform's marketing for free. Facebook doesn't care that you're outraged for the right reasons. The algorithm can't tell righteous anger from mob cruelty. It just sees engagement and serves you more.

Turn off every news notification on your phone. Not the annoying ones — all of them. No app needs real-time access to your attention. The news will still exist when you check it on your schedule, and you'll read it with a clearer head instead of reacting to whatever just happened in the last four minutes.

When you see someone getting destroyed online, don't add your voice to it. Not even to say you agree with the mob's target. Not even to make one small, reasonable point. The person is already done. Your contribution extends the suffering and adds another tick to the engagement counter. Close the tab.

Stop treating outrage as evidence of caring. The platforms trained you to believe that the angrier you get, the more you care about an issue. That's backwards. Rage is the cheapest emotional response you have. Calm, sustained attention to a problem is rarer and more valuable than fury that burns out in 48 hours.

If you find yourself compulsively checking for updates on a developing controversy, that's the rage machine working as designed. Break the loop by doing something that requires your hands — cook something, fix something, build something. The controversy will still be there. Your nervous system will thank you.

Follow the money when you feel outrage. Who profits when you're furious about this particular thing? Political fundraisers. Media companies with subscription models built on anxiety. Influencers whose brand depends on manufactured enemies. Before you share something that makes you angry, ask who gets paid.

Have one real political conversation per month with someone you genuinely disagree with, face to face. Not online, where you're performing for an audience. In person, where you're just two people trying to understand each other. It's harder, slower, and less satisfying than winning an argument on Twitter. It's also the only kind that ever actually changes anything.

Withdraw from platforms that are just rage dispensers. Reddit, in its current form, exists to make you feel superior and angry simultaneously. Twitter exists to create the fastest possible pipeline from thought to outrage. You don't need access to every human being's worst takes at all hours. You weren't designed for it.

The rage machine wins when you can't sit quietly for five minutes without reaching for your phone. Practice not reaching for it. The itch you feel is real — it's literally withdrawal from the dopamine loop they built. Let the itch be there. Don't scratch it.

Get angry about things you can actually affect. Local politics. Your own behavior. Things within your control. The internet specializes in routing your anger toward problems so large and distant that the only useful response it can generate is more content. Save the fury for things worth spending it on.

Chapter 2: Greed - The Attention Economy

You are not Facebook's customer. You are Facebook's product.

This isn't some clever internet meme. This is the literal business model of every major tech platform. They don't make money by selling you stuff. They make money by selling you to advertisers. Your attention, your data, your behavior, your deepest fears and desires get packaged up and sold to the highest bidder.

The phrase "surveillance capitalism" sounds dramatic, but it's exactly what's happening. These companies have built the most sophisticated spying operation in human history, and we pay them for the privilege of being watched.

Google knows more about you than your spouse does. They know what you search for at 3 AM when you can't sleep. They know your medical concerns, your financial problems, your relationship troubles. They know what you're thinking about buying before you know it yourself. All this data gets fed into advertising algorithms designed to manipulate your behavior.

Facebook tracks you even when you're not using Facebook. They have tracking pixels on millions of websites. They buy data from other companies about your offline purchases. They know where you shop, what you buy, who you talk to, where you go. They build "shadow profiles" on people who have never even signed up for their services.

Amazon's Alexa is always listening. Sure, they say it only records after you say the wake word, but how would you know? The device has to be listening constantly to hear the wake word in the first place. Amazon employees have admitted to listening to thousands of private conversations. Your bedroom talks, your arguments, your personal moments become data points.

The smartphone in your pocket is a tracking device making phone calls. It knows where you are every second of every day. It knows how fast you're moving, whether you're walking or driving, what apps you use when you're bored, anxious, or lonely. This location data gets sold to data brokers who package it up for advertisers, law enforcement, and anyone else willing to pay.

TikTok takes this to another level entirely. The app doesn't just track what you watch. It tracks how long you watch each video, when you pause, when you replay, what parts you skip. It reportedly analyzes your facial expressions through the front camera. It knows what makes you happy, sad, angry, or aroused. Then it feeds you more content designed to trigger those exact emotions.

The cryptocurrency boom was just another flavor of the same greed. Tech bros convinced millions of people digital coins backed by nothing were the future of money. They created artificial scarcity for digital assets costing nothing to produce. NFTs were even more absurd: paying thousands of dollars for a receipt saying you "own" a jpeg anyone can copy.

The whole crypto ecosystem was designed to extract money from regular people and funnel it to early adopters and exchange owners. Bitcoin mining consumed more electricity than entire countries while producing nothing of value. Ethereum gas fees made simple transactions cost hundreds of dollars. The environmental damage was massive, but the profits were bigger.

Social media turned human connection into a commodity. Your relationships became data points. Your conversations became training material for AI systems. Your photos became content for facial recognition databases. Your personal moments became advertising opportunities.

Instagram doesn't want you to feel good about yourself. They want you to feel just insecure enough to keep scrolling, keep posting, keep seeking validation through likes and comments. The data from your insecurity gets packaged and sold to companies wanting to exploit your vulnerabilities.

LinkedIn turned professional networking into performance art. Everyone became a thought leader sharing vapid inspirational posts designed to go viral. Real career advice got buried under a flood of humble-bragging and corporate cheerleading. The platform monetized workplace anxiety and professional insecurity.

Dating apps commodified love itself. Tinder turned human connection into a slot machine. Swipe, swipe, swipe, looking for that dopamine hit of a match. The apps make money by keeping you single and searching, not by helping you find lasting relationships. They sell premium features promising better matches while their algorithms ensure you never quite find what you're looking for.

The subscription economy trapped us in endless monthly payments. Software companies stopped selling products and started renting them. Adobe moved to subscription-only pricing, holding your creative work hostage unless you keep paying. Microsoft did the same with Office. Even car companies started charging monthly fees for features already built into vehicles you supposedly own.

Cloud storage became digital extortion. Google gives you just enough free storage to upload your entire life, then starts charging when you inevitably run out of space. Your photos, documents, and memories become leverage for ongoing payments. Try to leave, and you lose access to years of digital history.

The gig economy was sold as freedom but delivered digital sharecropping. Uber and Lyft drivers rent their cars to app companies while bearing all the costs and risks. DoorDash and Grubhub take huge cuts from restaurants and delivery drivers while producing nothing of value. Amazon Mechanical Turk pays people pennies for tasks generating millions in value.

These platforms extracted wealth from millions of workers while calling them independent contractors to avoid paying benefits or following labor laws. The "sharing economy" was really just the exploitation economy with better marketing.

App stores became digital toll booths. Apple takes 30% of every transaction on iOS, not because they add 30% of the value, but because they can. Google does the same on Android. Developers have no choice but to pay these fees if they want to reach smartphone users. The platforms hold entire industries hostage while skimming billions off the top.

The data economy turned human focus into a finite resource to be harvested and sold. Every notification, every autoplay video, every infinite scroll feature was designed to capture more of your mental bandwidth. The average person checks their phone 96 times per day because these devices were engineered to extract maximum data from every interaction.

Video games adopted casino mechanics to extract money from players. Loot boxes, battle passes, and in-app purchases turned gaming into gambling. Children got addicted to spending money on digital items that disappeared when the servers shut down. The industry made more money from addiction than from making good games.

News websites became clickbait factories optimized for advertising revenue. Headlines designed to make you angry or curious enough to click became more important than accurate reporting. Journalism died under an avalanche of sponsored content and programmatic advertising.

The promise of "free" services was always a lie. We paid with our privacy, our attention, our mental health, and our democracy. The true cost of these platforms is hidden in surveillance, manipulation, and the slow erosion of human agency.

Tech companies became more valuable than oil companies while producing nothing physical. They created artificial scarcity in infinite digital goods. They monetized human psychology and social connection. They turned our own behavior against us and called it innovation.

The greed isn't hidden. It's the entire point. Every feature, every update, every new platform is designed to extract more value from human attention and activity. We're not users. We're the raw material being processed by the surveillance economy machine.

What Do You Do About This?

Pay for your email. Gmail reads your messages to serve you ads — Google admitted this and only stopped after backlash, while continuing to analyze metadata. Fastmail and Proton Mail cost money. That money is why they're not selling you to advertisers. Pay it.

DuckDuckGo takes getting used to for about a week. After that, you won't miss Google Search for most queries. What you will miss is having your searches stored, analyzed, and used to build a profile of your fears, desires, and decision-making patterns. That profile is what you're giving up in exchange for slightly better results on obscure topics.

Install uBlock Origin in your browser right now. It blocks ads and the tracking scripts underneath them. Every page you load without it is a surveillance operation — dozens of third-party scripts recording where you clicked, how long you stayed, what you looked at. uBlock costs nothing and takes thirty seconds.

Stop giving apps your real phone number. Use Google Voice or a similar service for signups that require one. Your real number is attached to your identity in ways your email isn't. The fewer companies that have it, the fewer data brokers selling it to whoever pays.

Opt out of data broker sites. Companies like Whitepages, Spokeo, BeenVerified, and Intelius sell your home address, family members, income estimates, and personal history to anyone willing to pay. The opt-out process is intentionally tedious. Do it anyway.

Check what permissions your apps actually have. Most people have never done this. Open your phone settings and look at which apps have access to your location, microphone, camera, and contacts. You will find apps holding permissions they have no legitimate reason to have. Revoke them.

The 'free' business model is not neutral. Every free service is paid for by someone, and if you can't identify the customer, you're the product. This applies to apps, platforms, games, and news sites. The price of free is your data, your attention, and your psychological profile, sold to the highest bidder without your meaningful consent.

Credit cards track every purchase. This isn't paranoia — it's how credit card companies make money beyond interest. They sell transaction data to retailers, hedge funds, and marketers. Pay cash for purchases you'd prefer not to have analyzed. Not for illegal reasons. Because your spending habits are yours.

Delete apps you haven't used in sixty days. Every app on your phone is a potential surveillance point. Fewer apps watching you means less data harvested, fewer breach exposures, and a smaller footprint for companies trying to build a profile of your life.

The surveillance economy is built on your indifference. It survives because people find it easier to accept being watched than to spend thirty minutes on basic protections. Thirty minutes. That's the cost of meaningful privacy. Spend it.

Chapter 3: Envy - The Comparison Trap

Social media turned everyone into their own personal marketing department, and we're all failing at the job.

Every platform is designed to make you feel like you're not good enough. Your life isn't exciting enough. Your body isn't attractive enough. Your career isn't successful enough. Your relationships aren't happy enough. You're living your behind-the-scenes reality while watching everyone else's highlight reels.

The influencer economy is built on manufactured inadequacy. These people don't make money by being authentic. They make money by making you feel bad about yourself, then selling you products promising to fix your inadequacy. That fitness influencer didn't get those abs from the protein powder she's shilling. That lifestyle blogger didn't get rich from the productivity app she's promoting. They got rich by convincing you that you need what they're selling.

The FOMO epidemic spread like a virus. Fear of missing out became the dominant emotion of digital life. Every event you don't attend, every vacation you can't afford, every experience you haven't had gets rubbed in your face through carefully curated social media posts. Your friends aren't just living their lives anymore. They're performing their lives for an audience, and you're stuck watching from the cheap seats.

Vacation photos became weapons of mass depression. Every trip is documented and posted to make others jealous. The photos never show the flight delays, the food poisoning, the arguments, or the credit card debt. Just perfect sunsets and smiling faces designed to make everyone else feel like they're wasting their lives.

The home improvement craze on social media created impossible standards for domestic life. Every kitchen renovation, every perfectly organized closet, every aesthetically pleasing workspace became a reminder that your living space isn't good enough. People went into debt trying to recreate Pinterest-perfect homes for social media likes.

Parenting became a competitive sport played out on social media. Every milestone, every cute outfit, every educational activity got posted to prove what amazing parents people were. The pressure to document and perform parenthood made enjoying your children secondary to creating content about them.

Career success stories flooded professional networks with tales of rapid promotions, startup exits, and entrepreneurial victories. The failures, the rejections, the years of struggle never made it into the posts. Everyone appeared to be succeeding at life while you were stuck in your mediocre job wondering what you were doing wrong.

Fitness culture became about showing off rather than staying healthy. Every workout, every protein shake, every before-and-after photo was designed to demonstrate superiority over people who weren't as dedicated to their physical transformation. The gym became a photo studio where people spent more time documenting their workouts than exercising.

Food photography turned meals into status symbols. Every restaurant visit, every home-cooked dinner, every artisanal coffee became an opportunity to show off your refined taste and disposable income. People stopped enjoying their food and started performing their eating habits for social media validation.

Shopping hauls became a way to flaunt wealth and taste. Unboxing videos and closet tours showed off designer purchases and trendy acquisitions. The message was clear: your wardrobe, your gadgets, your possessions weren't good enough compared to what these people could afford.

Beauty standards became completely divorced from reality. Filters and editing apps let people completely transform their appearance before posting photos. Young people developed body dysmorphia trying to look like digitally altered versions of influencers who don't even look like their own photos.

The wellness industry exploited this comparison culture ruthlessly. Every smoothie bowl, yoga pose, and meditation session became content designed to make others feel spiritually inadequate. "Self-care" became performance art where people competed to show how much better they were at taking care of themselves than you were.

Everyone became a brand, and most of us are failing brands. We're all trying to market ourselves as successful, attractive, interesting people while feeling like frauds behind the carefully curated facade. The pressure to maintain a perfect online presence became a full-time job that nobody applied for.

The promise was connection and community. The reality is isolation and inadequacy. Social media doesn't make us feel more connected to others. It makes us feel worse about ourselves while watching other people perform better versions of life than the one we're living.

What Do You Do About This?

Stop following anyone whose job is to make you want things. Influencers are salespeople. Their entire function is to create desire in you for things you didn't know you needed until they showed up in your feed. The life they're selling is a product, and you're the market. Follow people who make things or know things. Stop following people who simply have things.

Delete Instagram from your phone and access it only through a browser if you use it at all. The app is specifically engineered to maximize time-on-platform through comparison triggers. The web version works fine for keeping up with actual friends and is far less effective at making you feel inadequate. That's the point.

The person you're comparing yourself to is comparing themselves to someone else. The fitness influencer with the impossible body is looking at someone with a better body. The entrepreneur posting about startup success is quietly terrified of someone else's bigger success. The comparison chain goes all the way up and it never ends. You joined a game you can't win.

Document less. When you're at dinner, on vacation, or doing something you enjoy, put the phone face down. Not to post later — just to experience the thing without narrating it. The reflex to document everything is a product of social media. Your brain learned to process experiences as potential content. Unlearn it.

Before you buy anything you saw online, wait 48 hours. The influencer economy runs on impulse purchases driven by manufactured desire. The product will still exist in two days. Your need for it usually won't survive the wait. This one rule will save you money you don't have to spend on things you don't actually want.

Unfollow people in your real life who consistently make you feel bad. This includes people you like in person. Social media versions of people you know are their carefully curated highlight reels too. You don't have to sit for the performance.

Track your own progress against your past self only. Where were you a year ago? Six months ago? That's the only comparison that gives you useful information. Comparing yourself to strangers with different resources, different starting points, and different goals tells you nothing useful and costs you peace of mind.

When you feel the comparison pull, write down three things that are specifically good about your actual life right now. Not platitudes — specific things. The brain that's been trained to scan for what you lack can be deliberately redirected toward what you have. It won't happen automatically. You have to force it. Do it anyway.

The comparison trap is a business model. Platforms don't accidentally make you feel bad — they engineer it. The mild, chronic anxiety from scrolling is what keeps you there, seeking relief. The relief never comes from the platform. It comes from closing it.

Understand what you're actually envying. Usually it's not the vacation or the body or the career — it's the feeling those things represent. Safety. Freedom. Control. Those feelings are available to you from sources that don't require performing your life for strangers online.

Chapter 4: Pride - The Echo Chamber

The internet convinced everyone they're a genius, and now we're all trapped in rooms full of mirrors reflecting our own opinions back at us.

Everyone became an expert overnight. Got a Google search? You're now qualified to debate doctors about medical treatments. Watched a YouTube video? You understand climate science better than researchers who spent decades studying it. Read a blog post? You're ready to lecture economists about monetary policy.

The democratization of information was supposed to make us smarter. Instead, it made us more arrogant. Having access to all human knowledge at our fingertips didn't create a generation of scholars. It created a generation of people who confused having opinions with having expertise.

Wikipedia made everyone feel like they understood complex topics after reading a few paragraphs. People started citing Wikipedia articles in debates as if they'd conducted original research. The ability to quickly look up facts got confused with actually understanding those facts in context.

Google Scholar turned everyone into their own research department. People learned to find studies supporting whatever position they already held while ignoring the broader scientific consensus. Cherry-picking became the dominant form of intellectual inquiry. Why read systematic reviews when you can find one study that confirms your bias?

The self-help industry exploded because everyone became convinced they could solve any problem with the right mindset. Motivational speakers promised that positive thinking could cure disease, attract wealth, and guarantee success. Personal development became a substitute for acknowledging that some problems require expertise, luck, or systemic change.

Cryptocurrency culture bred a special form of intellectual arrogance. People who bought Bitcoin at the right time became convinced they understood economics better than Nobel Prize winners. Day traders who got lucky during bull markets started giving financial advice to millions of followers. Making money in a bubble became proof of investment genius.

The DIY movement went from practical skills to dangerous overconfidence. YouTube tutorials convinced people they could perform their own electrical work, diagnose their own medical conditions, and represent themselves in legal proceedings. Having access to information became confused with having the competence to act on that information.

Podcast culture created armchair philosophers who confused listening to conversations with developing expertise. People who consumed hundreds of hours of Joe Rogan or Tim Ferriss started believing they understood neuroscience, nutrition, and human optimization. Passive consumption of content became mistaken for active learning.

Stock market forums turned amateur investors into financial gurus. Reddit communities like WallStreetBets convinced people that traditional investment advice was obsolete. Meme stocks and diamond hands became substitute strategies for understanding market fundamentals. Gambling became investing, and losing money became a badge of honor.

Parenting blogs made every parent an expert on child development. People who read attachment theory articles started lecturing pediatricians about infant care. Pinterest boards replaced professional guidance. Mommy bloggers became more trusted sources than child psychologists.

Fitness influencers convinced their followers that six-pack abs qualified them to dispense medical advice. Personal trainers started diagnosing autoimmune conditions and prescribing supplements. Transformation photos became credentials for understanding human physiology.

The hustle culture movement made everyone a business strategist. People who made money selling courses about making money became entrepreneurship experts. Having a side hustle qualified you to lecture others about building wealth. Success stories replaced business education.

Spiritual communities fragmented into countless micro-gurus each claiming unique insights into consciousness and reality. Everyone who had a psychedelic experience became a philosopher. Meditation apps turned mindfulness practice into another area where people competed to demonstrate their enlightenment.

Travel bloggers convinced their audiences they understood geopolitics because they'd visited different countries. A few weeks backpacking through Southeast Asia qualified someone to explain cultural differences and economic development. Tourism became anthropology.

Food culture turned everyone into nutritionists. People who tried elimination diets became qualified to diagnose food sensitivities in others. Home cooks started lecturing about the health effects of different cooking methods. Personal anecdotes became nutritional science.

The problem isn't that people are curious or want to learn. The problem is that the internet made it impossible to distinguish between having information and having understanding, between exposure and expertise, between opinions and knowledge.

Everyone became their own authority on everything, and expertise became just another opinion competing for attention in the marketplace of ideas. The difference between amateur enthusiasm and professional competence disappeared in a sea of confident assertions and viral content.

The tragedy is that real learning requires intellectual humility. It requires acknowledging what you don't know, respecting the complexity of difficult subjects, and understanding that expertise takes time to develop. The internet made us feel smart while making us actually more ignorant.

What Do You Do About This?

Your opinions are downstream of your information sources. If every source you consume reaches the same conclusions, you don't have opinions — you have programming. The test of a real position isn't whether you can defend it to people who already agree with you. It's whether it survives the strongest version of the counterargument.

Read the primary source. Not the article about the study. Not the tweet about the article about the study. The actual study, paper, or document. Academic papers are publicly available. Government reports are public record. Most of the time, the primary source says something significantly different from what the outrage machine made of it.

Find the best commentator on the opposing side of any issue you care about. Not the most extreme — the most intelligent. If you can't find an intelligent version of the opposing view, you haven't looked hard enough. The absence of intelligent opposition in your information diet is a sign of an echo chamber, not a sign that you're right.

Wikipedia is the beginning of research, not the end of it. The citations at the bottom of a Wikipedia article lead to actual sources. Go there. Most people treat Wikipedia as authoritative and never follow a single citation. That's how you end up confidently wrong about things you've never actually studied.

Change your mind publicly sometimes. When you encounter evidence that shifts your view, say so. People who never visibly change their minds are either performing certainty or not doing the intellectual work. Real thinking produces position changes. Show the work.

Be specific about what you know versus what you believe. 'I think' and 'studies show' are not the same thing. 'I read one article that suggested' and 'the scientific consensus is' are not the same thing. Precision about the basis for your claims is not weakness. It's accuracy.

The algorithm feeds you what confirms your existing views because confirmed views produce more engagement than challenged ones. You feel good when you read you're right. The platforms are not in the business of making you smarter. They're in the business of making you comfortable enough to stay.

Talk to people in fields you know nothing about and just listen. Not to debate them. To understand what expertise in that field actually looks and sounds like. Most people who think they understand complex fields have never spent a real hour with someone who spent years in those fields. Do that before forming strong opinions.

Expertise is narrow. Even genuine experts are only expert in their specific area. A virologist's opinions on economic policy deserve the same skepticism as an economist's opinions on virology. Credentials transfer badly. Evaluate claims on their merits, not the source's general reputation.

The echo chamber feels like clarity. It feels like finally being around people who get it. That feeling is the warning sign. Intellectual comfort is not the same as intellectual accuracy. Get uncomfortable deliberately.

Chapter 5: Lust - Digital Desire Gone Wrong

The internet turned human sexuality into a commodity, and now we're all customers in the world's largest strip club that never closes.

Pornography used to require effort to obtain. You had to drive somewhere, make eye contact with a cashier, hide magazines under your mattress. The internet eliminated all friction between sexual desire and instant gratification. Now hardcore pornography is three clicks away from any child with a smartphone, and we're all pretending this is fine.

The average age of first pornography exposure is now eleven years old. Children are learning about sexuality from content designed to appeal to adult male fantasies. They're developing expectations about bodies, performance, and relationships based on material created by an industry that profits from degradation and unrealistic scenarios.

OnlyFans monetized intimate relationships by turning ordinary people into pornography producers. The platform convinced young women that selling sexual content to strangers was empowerment rather than exploitation. Subscribers paid for personalized attention and fake intimacy while creators performed emotional labor disguised as sexual liberation.

Parasocial relationships exploded across streaming platforms. People developed one-sided emotional connections with streamers and content creators who didn't know they existed. Twitch viewers donated thousands of dollars to female gamers hoping for personal acknowledgment. Fans felt genuine heartbreak when their favorite creators got married or started dating someone else.

The cam girl industry industrialized fake intimacy. Performers learned to make every viewer feel special and uniquely appreciated while simultaneously entertaining dozens of other paying customers. Men paid premium prices for the illusion of personal connection with women who were following scripts designed to maximize spending.

The industry depends on that illusion holding. Most of the time it does, in the sense that most users don't commit violence. What they do instead is spend. Cam site addiction follows the same arc as every other compulsive behavior the internet enables: the amounts escalate, the user hides it, the money runs out, and then they find more money — from savings, from credit cards, from family members who don't know what they're funding, sometimes from theft. Men have bankrupted themselves. Men have stolen from their employers, their parents, their children's college funds. The addiction is chemically identical to gambling addiction — variable reinforcement, the illusion of a relationship with the machine, the belief that the next session will be different. A man in the American Midwest took it further. He spent years paying a cam model in Bulgaria. She was professional, attentive, made him feel like the relationship was real. For him, it was. He believed they had something exclusive. When he needed more money to keep it going — the payments were substantial, ongoing, and growing — his family was in the way. He murdered them. The model had no idea he existed as anything other than a username and a payment source. She was doing her job. He had confused her job for a relationship, and that confusion had a body count. Murder is the extreme end. Financial ruin is the common end. The industry constructs both outcomes from the same raw material: the systematic simulation of personal intimacy sold to men who cannot maintain the boundary between what they are buying and what they believe.

The women on the other side of the screen are their own category of victim, and the industry works hard to keep them invisible. Romania, Bulgaria, and other Eastern European countries with high unemployment and few economic options for women supply a significant share of the cam industry's workforce. The choice, for many of them, is not between camming and a career. It is between camming and the streets. That is not a choice. That is coercion with extra steps. Beyond the economic pressure, a substantial portion of cam performers are not working for themselves. They are working for someone who recruited them, controls their schedule, takes most of the money, and keeps them in place through debt, threats, and the kind of fear that doesn't need to be stated out loud to be effective. The platforms know this. They do not ask. The terms of service that prohibit trafficking are not enforced in any meaningful way because enforcement would reduce supply, and reduced supply would reduce revenue. The woman performing for a paying audience of strangers, looking attentive and available and exclusively focused on whoever is watching — she may be doing this because she chose to. She may be doing this because someone decided she would. The viewer cannot tell the difference. The platform does not try to find out.

Virtual reality pornography promised to make fantasy indistinguishable from reality. Companies developed haptic feedback devices synchronized with VR content to simulate physical sensation. The technology aimed to replace human sexual connection with perfectly controllable digital experiences tailored to individual preferences.

AI girlfriend apps provided companionship without the complications of actual relationships. Users could design their perfect partner's appearance, personality, and sexual preferences without dealing with the messy realities of human emotion and autonomy. The apps promised love without effort, intimacy without vulnerability, and satisfaction without reciprocity.

Sexting became the dominant form of teenage sexual exploration. Kids who had never held hands were exchanging explicit photos and messages. The permanent digital record of these conversations created new forms of sexual exploitation where private moments became public humiliation or blackmail material.

Revenge porn weaponized intimate images as tools of harassment and control. Ex-partners published private photos and videos to punish former lovers, destroy reputations, and maintain psychological dominance. The internet's permanent memory turned private intimate moments into lifetime scarlet letters.

Deepfake technology made it possible to create realistic pornographic videos of anyone using just a few photos. Celebrities, politicians, classmates, and ex-partners could be digitally inserted into explicit content without their consent. The technology democratized a new form of sexual assault that required no physical contact.

Live streaming platforms became hunting grounds for sexual predators targeting children. Adults used gaming platforms, social media, and video chat services to groom minors for sexual exploitation. The technology designed to connect people became a tool for the worst forms of abuse.

Sugar daddy websites normalized transactional relationships disguised as mentorship. Older men paid younger women for "companionship" while both parties pretended the financial arrangement wasn't prostitution. The platforms provided legal cover for sex work while avoiding the regulations and protections that actual sex workers needed.

Escort services moved online and rebranded as "companion" services. Apps and websites connected sex workers with clients while maintaining plausible deniability about the nature of the transactions. The digital marketplace made sex trafficking easier to hide and harder to regulate.

The porn industry shaped sexual expectations for an entire generation. Young people learned that women should be perpetually available, enthusiastic about any sexual act, and physically perfect. They learned that men should be dominant, emotionally distant, and capable of marathon sexual performance. Reality couldn't compete with fantasy.

Fetish communities found new ways to exploit vulnerable people through online platforms. Financial domination, where submissives sent money to dominants for humiliation, moved from niche kink to mainstream exploitation. People with psychological vulnerabilities became ATM machines for predators who understood how to manipulate shame and desire.

Sex robots promised to eliminate the need for human sexual partners entirely. Companies developed increasingly realistic dolls with artificial intelligence, responsive skin, and programmable personalities. The technology aimed to provide sexual satisfaction without the complications of human emotion, consent, or mutual pleasure.

The attention economy sexualized childhood by rewarding young people for increasingly provocative content. Dance challenges on TikTok became more suggestive. Instagram photos became more revealing. The platforms rewarded sexual content with views and engagement while young users learned that their value came from their ability to attract sexual attention.

The internet promised to liberate human sexuality from shame and repression. Instead, it commercialized intimate human connection and turned sexual desire into another vector for exploitation, addiction, and alienation. We got infinite sexual content but lost the ability to connect sexually with actual human beings.

What Do You Do About This?

Have a direct, specific conversation with yourself about what pornography has done to your expectations. Are your expectations of partners realistic? Have you noticed decreasing interest in real-world intimacy? Has your tolerance shifted toward increasingly extreme content? These are not rhetorical questions. Answer them honestly before deciding you don't have a problem.

Age verification for pornography is not an infringement on adult freedom. Children are currently accessing hardcore content as easily as they access YouTube. Every country that has implemented serious age verification has seen measurable reductions in child exposure. Support it. The inconvenience to adults is minor. The protection for children is not.

If you consume pornography, at least make it ethically produced. Subscription platforms with verified performers are less likely to host exploitation than free tube sites that pay nobody and verify nothing. The free tube site model exists partly because piracy destroyed the legitimate adult industry and partly because unverified content is cheaper to host.

Dating apps have turned human attraction into a sorting algorithm. The swiping mechanic trains your brain to evaluate people the same way you evaluate products. You will not meet someone who's genuinely good for you through rapid-fire visual screening of hundreds of profiles. The psychological damage from the process is real regardless of outcome.

The loneliness that drives excessive pornography use or compulsive digital sexual behavior doesn't get solved by more pornography or more apps. It gets solved by vulnerability with real people — which is the thing that digital sex culture is specifically designed to avoid requiring. Real intimacy is risky. That's what makes it worth having.

If you have children, they will encounter pornography before you think they will. The average age of first exposure is eleven. They will encounter it before you've had any conversation about it. Have the conversation now, before the algorithm has it for you. Be specific about what pornography is, what it isn't, and why the two things are different.

Revenge porn — non-consensual intimate imagery — is illegal in most US states and many countries. If you've ever shared or considered sharing intimate images of someone without their consent, stop. If it's happened to you, organizations like the Cyber Civil Rights Initiative have resources specifically for this. Report it rather than absorbing it as a private humiliation.

OnlyFans and the creator economy around digital sexuality have convinced many young people that selling sexual content is entrepreneurship. For some adults making fully informed choices, it may be. For many, it's desperation monetized by a platform that takes 20% and leaves creators with permanent reputational consequences they didn't fully calculate in advance.

Digital desire is engineered. The platforms that host it are engineered. The psychological responses they exploit are real biological vulnerabilities. Knowing that won't make you immune. But it should change the weight you give to impulses that arrive via screen.

Human sexual connection requires vulnerability, communication, and mutual respect. Technology can enable connection but cannot replicate the fundamental human need for intimacy with another person who sees you as a full human being rather than a delivery mechanism for fantasy.

Chapter 6: Gluttony - Information Overconsumption

The internet promised to give us all the information we could ever want. It delivered. Now we're drowning in it.

We went from information scarcity to information obesity in less than a generation. Our brains evolved to seek out new information because it used to be rare and valuable. Now we're surrounded by an infinite buffet of content, and we can't stop consuming even though it's making us sick.

A 2011 study estimated the average person was already consuming the equivalent of 174 newspapers' worth of information daily — five times more than in 1986. That was fifteen years ago, before TikTok, before Reels, before AI-generated content flooded every feed. Our brains weren't designed to process this much input. We're cognitive hoarders living in digital houses packed floor to ceiling with useless information we'll never need.

News websites became content factories optimized for maximum consumption rather than informed citizenship. Every minor event became "breaking news." Every celebrity tweet became a story. Every political statement became a crisis requiring immediate attention. The 24-hour news cycle stretched into a 24-second attention cycle where yesterday's emergency was already forgotten.

Social media feeds became bottomless wells of content designed to keep you scrolling forever. The infinite scroll eliminated natural stopping points that might let you realize you'd consumed enough. There's always one more post, one more video, one more update waiting to capture your attention.

Podcast addiction replaced radio for the intellectually curious. People binged entire series in single sessions, consuming hundreds of hours of content about productivity, philosophy, and self-improvement without implementing any of it. The feeling of learning became a substitute for learning.

Information FOMO created anxiety about missing important updates. People checked news sites obsessively, afraid that something significant might happen while they weren't paying attention. The fear of being uninformed drove compulsive information consumption that left people feeling overwhelmed rather than educated.

The paradox of choice paralyzed decision-making. Streaming services with thousands of movies left people unable to pick what to watch. Online courses with unlimited options made choosing education feel impossible. Information abundance created decision fatigue instead of better choices.

Digital hoarding replaced physical hoarding for the internet generation. People saved thousands of articles they'd never read, bookmarked hundreds of videos they'd never watch, and subscribed to dozens of newsletters they'd never open. The possibility of future consumption became more important than present enjoyment.

Content creators learned to hack attention spans by delivering rapid-fire information designed to feel educational while requiring no real effort. "Productivity porn" videos promised to teach you everything about complex topics in ten minutes or less. The feeling of learning replaced the work of learning.

Email newsletters multiplied like spam as every expert, influencer, and content creator launched their own publication. People subscribed to dozens of daily newsletters, creating inbox anxiety and information overwhelm. The fear of missing out on valuable insights led to consuming far more information than anyone could meaningfully process.

Speed reading courses and summarization services promised to help people consume more information faster without addressing whether consuming more information was helpful. The solution to information overload became consuming information more efficiently instead of consuming less information more thoughtfully.

Documentary streaming became intellectual binge-eating. People watched dozens of documentaries about social issues, historical events, and scientific discoveries while taking no action based on what they learned. Passive consumption of educational content replaced active engagement with important topics.

Online course addiction affected people who enrolled in hundreds of classes without completing any of them. The excitement of starting new learning projects became more appealing than the work of finishing existing ones. Digital learning platforms enabled educational gluttony disguised as self-improvement.

RSS feeds and news aggregators let people subscribe to hundreds of information sources, creating personalized information firehoses that delivered more content than anyone could reasonably consume. The technology supposed to help manage information overload made it worse by removing friction from information consumption.

Audio content exploded as people tried to multitask their way through information consumption. Audiobooks, podcasts, and educational videos played constantly in the background while people worked, exercised, and commuted. The idea of silence or mental downtime became uncomfortable for brains addicted to constant input.

Wikipedia became the intellectual equivalent of fast food. People gorged themselves on shallow summaries of complex topics, convincing themselves they understood subjects after reading a few paragraphs. The depth and nuance of real expertise got flattened into digestible snippets that satisfied curiosity without providing real knowledge.

Live streaming turned watching other people's lives into entertainment. People spent hours watching strangers play video games, cook meals, or just talk to their cameras. Parasocial relationships with streamers replaced real social interaction while consuming massive amounts of time and attention.

Comment sections became information landfills where people dumped half-formed thoughts and random reactions. Reading comments became a compulsive behavior that added no value but consumed endless time. The human need for social interaction got satisfied by consuming strangers' opinions about articles, videos, and posts.

Browser tabs multiplied like weeds as people opened article after article without finishing any of them. Twenty, thirty, fifty tabs remained open as monuments to good intentions and information anxiety. The fear of losing potentially valuable information prevented people from ever actually consuming the information they'd saved.

News aggregation apps promised to solve information overload by curating content from multiple sources. Instead, they created meta-feeds that delivered even more information to consume. The cure for too much information became more information delivered more efficiently.

Social media algorithms learned to serve addictive information cocktails tailored to individual psychological profiles. Each person got a personalized blend of content designed to keep them engaged, angry, or anxious enough to keep consuming. The information diet became as individualized and unhealthy as junk food.

Trivia knowledge replaced deep understanding as the goal of information consumption. People collected random facts like baseball cards, prioritizing breadth over depth. Knowing a little about everything became more valued than knowing a lot about anything important.

Information became a drug with diminishing returns. People needed increasingly frequent hits of new content to feel satisfied. The dopamine hit from discovering interesting information became addictive, leading to compulsive information-seeking behavior that interfered with sleep, work, and relationships.

We replaced wisdom with Google searches and deep thinking with shallow browsing. The internet gave us access to all human knowledge, but we used it to become less knowledgeable than ever. We confused having information with understanding information, consuming content with learning from content.

The promise was enlightenment through unlimited access to information. The reality is cognitive overload from consuming far more than we can meaningfully process. We're information gluttons in a world that mistakes consumption for nourishment.

What Do You Do About This?

You are not obligated to have an opinion about everything that happens. The news cycle generates one crisis per day specifically because that's what keeps you returning. Most of those crises will be forgotten within a week. The permanent background hum of catastrophe is a product of the content business, not an accurate representation of how fast the world is actually changing.

Pick two or three news sources and read those only. Not twenty. Not whatever shows up in your feed. Algorithmic news delivery is designed to maximize emotional response, not informational quality. Deliberately selected sources read on your schedule are a fundamentally different experience than algorithmic feeds.

Stop checking news in the morning before you've done anything else. The first hour of the day sets your cognitive baseline. Starting it with an anxiety injection from your news feed means spending the most productive hours of your day processing information you didn't need yet. Read the news after you've done something.

If you've read the same type of article ten times this month — another political outrage, another study about food, another celebrity conflict — you can safely skip the next one. You already know what it says. More of the same information does not make you better informed. It makes you more anxious.

Newsletters are not the solution to too much content. They are additional content. Every newsletter you subscribe to was designed to feel more curated and meaningful than the feed it's supposed to replace. Most are just more tabs you feel guilty about not opening. Unsubscribe ruthlessly from anything you haven't read in a month.

Long-form reading — actual books, long magazine features, academic papers — builds the cognitive capacity that social media erodes. You're not better informed from reading five hundred short articles than from reading three books. You have more exposure and less understanding. Understanding requires sustained attention. Sustained attention requires practice.

The feeling that you need to stay current on everything is manufactured. Financial media needs you anxious about markets. Political media needs you anxious about elections. Health media needs you anxious about your body. They are not providing information service. They are selling anxiety with a news wrapper.

Information you can't act on is just weight. News about things happening in countries you've never been to, involving people you'll never meet, that you have no capacity to affect, is not making you a better citizen of the world. Constrain your information diet to things you can actually do something with.

Take at least one full day per week away from news consumption. The world will not fall apart during the 24 hours you're not watching. What you'll discover is that catching up the next day takes about fifteen minutes. Which tells you something about how much of what you were consuming was necessary.

Your attention is finite. Every hour spent consuming information is an hour not spent creating, connecting, or being present in the physical world. The information gluttony the internet makes possible is not free. It's paid for with the hours of your actual life.

Chapter 7: Sloth - The Death of Effort

Technology promised to make our lives easier. Mission accomplished. Now we can't do anything the hard way, and we're forgetting how to do anything at all.

Calculators eliminated basic math skills. Students can't calculate tips, figure out discounts, or estimate costs without pulling out their phones. Mental arithmetic became as obsolete as slide rules. People who can't multiply single digits in their heads somehow convinced themselves they don't need math because they have technology.

Google turned us into externally dependent thinkers. Instead of remembering information, we remember where to find information. Phone numbers, addresses, historical dates, and basic facts all got outsourced to search engines. Our brains became lazy because Google was always there to do the work.

Spell check destroyed our ability to write without technological assistance. Auto-correct became a crutch that enabled illiteracy disguised as efficiency. People stopped learning proper spelling and grammar because their devices would fix mistakes automatically. Take away the red squiggly lines, and most people write like they never learned to spell.

Ride-sharing apps eliminated the need to plan transportation. People stopped checking bus schedules, learning subway maps, or figuring out how to get places independently. They became helpless without Uber, unable to navigate their own cities using public transportation or their own two feet.

Food delivery services made cooking optional. DoorDash and Grubhub convinced people that spending three times the cost of groceries for restaurant meals delivered to their door was normal behavior. Kitchens became decorative spaces while people lost the basic skill of cooking for themselves.

Video tutorials replaced hands-on learning and problem-solving skills. People expected step-by-step instructions for everything instead of figuring things out through trial and error.

The ability to troubleshoot, adapt, and improvise atrophied because YouTube always had a video showing exactly what to do.

Customer service chatbots trained people to expect instant solutions to every problem. The tolerance for working through difficulties, waiting for resolution, or solving problems independently disappeared. Everything had to be fixed immediately with minimal effort, or people gave up entirely.

Streaming services removed the effort required to choose entertainment. Recommendation engines suggested what to watch based on viewing history, eliminating the need to browse, research, or discover new content independently. People became passive consumers who couldn't decide what they wanted to watch without algorithmic assistance.

Photo editing apps made everyone a professional photographer without learning photography skills. Filters, automatic adjustments, and AI enhancement meant people never learned about lighting, composition, or camera settings. The instant gratification of perfect photos replaced the satisfaction of developing technical expertise.

Voice assistants eliminated the need to remember schedules, set alarms, or manage basic tasks. Alexa and Siri became external brains that handled reminders, appointments, and simple calculations. People lost the ability to organize their own lives without digital assistance.

Password managers made remembering login credentials unnecessary. While this solved security problems, it also meant people couldn't access their own accounts without technological assistance. Digital dependency extended to the most basic requirement of proving your identity online.

Translation apps eliminated the motivation to learn foreign languages. Why spend years studying Spanish when Google Translate could handle conversations instantly? The effort required for real bilingual fluency seemed pointless when technology provided good-enough communication.

E-readers and audiobooks reduced the mental effort required for reading. Features like adjustable font sizes, built-in dictionaries, and variable playback speeds made consuming books easier but also reduced the cognitive workout that comes from wrestling with challenging text at normal speed.

Online shopping with one-click purchasing removed the friction that might make people reconsider unnecessary purchases. The effort of going to stores, comparing prices, and thinking about purchases got eliminated in favor of instant gratification that encouraged impulsive spending.

Email templates and auto-responses reduced personal communication to form letters. People stopped writing thoughtful messages because suggested replies and canned responses were faster and easier. Authentic communication became too much work when technology could handle most interactions automatically.

Fitness tracking apps promised to motivate exercise but often replaced actual physical activity with the illusion of progress. People became more focused on closing rings and hitting step goals than developing real fitness, strength, or athletic skills. Gamification substituted for genuine physical achievement.

AI writing assistants started doing homework, emails, and creative work for people. Students used ChatGPT to write essays without learning writing skills. Professionals used AI to draft communications without developing their own voice. The technology meant to enhance human capability began replacing human effort entirely.

Smart home devices automated every basic household task from adjusting temperature to turning on lights. People lost the ability to operate their own homes without voice commands and smartphone apps. Basic mechanical skills and environmental awareness disappeared when everything became app-controlled.

Assembly instructions disappeared as furniture and electronics became increasingly complex and user-hostile. Companies designed products that required professional installation or specialized tools, eliminating the satisfaction and skill-building that comes from assembling things yourself. The DIY culture died when everything became too complicated for normal people to fix or build.

Automatic bill pay and financial management apps eliminated the need to understand personal finances. People stopped tracking spending, balancing checkbooks, or understanding where their money went each month. Financial literacy became optional when apps could handle budgeting and payments automatically.

Calendar apps with automatic scheduling removed the mental effort of time management. People stopped planning their days, estimating how long tasks would take, or developing time awareness. Digital assistants handled scheduling conflicts and reminders, leaving users unable to manage their own time without technological support.

Weather apps eliminated the skill of reading natural signs and patterns. People stopped noticing cloud formations, wind changes, or seasonal patterns because their phones provided detailed forecasts. The ability to observe and interpret the natural world atrophied when all environmental information came from screens.

The promise was liberation from tedious tasks so we could focus on more important work. The reality is learned helplessness where people can't function without technological assistance. We optimized for convenience and accidentally eliminated competence.

Every skill we outsourced to technology made us more dependent and less capable. The devices that were supposed to help us instead made us helpless. We traded self-reliance for efficiency and discovered that efficiency without capability is just sophisticated incompetence.

The sloth the internet created isn't laziness. It's something more insidious: a systematic replacement of competence with dependency, engineered by companies that profit from your helplessness. Every skill you lose to convenience becomes a subscription they can sell back to you. Every capability you outsource becomes a point of control. This wasn't an accident of progress. It was the business model.

What Do You Do About This?

Turn off GPS for any trip under twenty minutes. Navigate. Use the map in your head, stop and look at a posted sign, or ask someone. You will be slower and occasionally wrong. You will also develop or maintain the spatial reasoning that GPS navigation is actively replacing. Your brain needs exercise the same way your body does, and outsourcing navigation is one of the most consistent ways we've collectively stopped doing it.

Memorize ten phone numbers. Not contacts — actual numbers you know by heart. Your spouse, your parents, your closest friend, your doctor. If your phone is stolen or dead, you should be able to call someone. Most people currently know zero numbers beyond their own. This is a specific skill that's completely disappeared in one generation.

Do math with a pencil sometimes. Not for complex problems — basic arithmetic. Tips, percentages, time estimates. The calculator has made this feel unnecessary, and it is unnecessary if you only care about the answer. But mental arithmetic keeps certain cognitive pathways active. Use them or lose them.

Cook without a recipe once a week. Understand what's in your refrigerator and make something from it. Recipe apps have made people better at following instructions and worse at understanding food. Knowing how to cook improves with understanding — how heat works, how flavors combine, what techniques accomplish. Following a recipe is reading. Actually cooking is knowing.

Write by hand regularly. Notes, letters, journaling — something. Handwriting engages different cognitive processes than typing, including memory consolidation. Students who handwrite notes consistently outperform those who type on factual recall. The mechanics of formation slow you down enough to process what you're writing.

Fix something before you replace it. Know how your basic tools work. Learn to change a tire, reset a circuit breaker, unclog a drain, fix a bicycle flat. Not because you'll always need to — because understanding mechanical reality makes you more competent, more confident, and less dependent on the assumption that someone else will always be available.

Read paper books specifically. Not because e-readers are bad, but because paper books don't send notifications, don't contain other books, and don't connect to the internet. The reason attention spans have shortened is specifically the competition for attention within the device. Remove the device from the reading experience.

Learn to be bored productively. Boredom used to be when humans did their actual thinking — staring out windows, letting the mind wander, making connections between things. The smartphone eliminated boredom entirely and replaced it with endless low-level stimulation. Let yourself be bored for thirty minutes. Notice what happens.

Stop outsourcing your opinions. When you need a restaurant, a plumber, a book, or a film, make a decision based on your own knowledge and preferences before checking what the algorithm recommends. Your taste is not worse for being yours. The recommendation economy benefits from you not trusting yourself.

Convenience is a loan you take against your own capability. Every time technology does something for you, you're betting that the technology will always be available and functional. When it isn't — no GPS in the dead zone, no signal for the app you need — you discover exactly what you've borrowed and not paid back.

Chapter 8: Deception - The Age of Unreality

The internet was supposed to be the ultimate truth machine, giving everyone access to facts and information. Instead, it became the most powerful lie amplifier in human history.

We live in an age where seeing is no longer believing, but people believe everything they see online anyway. The same technology that democratized information also democratized deception. Anyone with a laptop can now produce lies that look more convincing than the truth.

Social media turned everyone into a propaganda publisher. People share articles without reading them, spread rumors without verifying them, and amplify false stories without understanding them. The platforms reward engagement over accuracy, so lies that provoke strong emotional reactions spread faster than boring truths.

Photoshop and photo editing apps made visual evidence unreliable. Every image can be manipulated, enhanced, or completely fabricated. People lost the ability to distinguish between authentic photos and digital creations, but they kept treating edited images as documentary evidence of events that never happened.

Fake news websites masqueraded as legitimate journalism while publishing completely fabricated stories. Sites with official-sounding names like "American News Today" or "National Report" created made-up articles designed to confirm people's existing beliefs and generate advertising revenue through viral sharing.

Catfishing became so common that online relationships required constant verification. People created entirely fictional identities using stolen photos and fabricated life stories. Romance scammers built emotional connections with victims over months before revealing their true financial motives. The internet made it easier to fall in love with someone who didn't exist than to trust someone who did.

Astroturfing campaigns created the illusion of grassroots movements using armies of fake accounts. Companies, governments, and political organizations hired firms to generate artificial support for their positions using bots and paid commenters. Real public opinion became impossible to distinguish from manufactured consensus.

Identity theft moved beyond financial fraud to complete life impersonation. Criminals used social media information to assume victims' identities online, opening accounts, making purchases, and even maintaining relationships using stolen personas. People discovered their digital lives had been hijacked by strangers living parallel lives in their name.

Email scams evolved from obvious Nigerian prince schemes to sophisticated phishing operations targeting specific people with personalized information. Spear phishing attacks used social media research to create convincing messages that appeared to come from trusted friends, colleagues, or family members.

Academic paper mills produced fake research studies for hire. Companies wanting to support their products with scientific evidence could purchase fraudulent studies published in predatory journals that looked legitimate but had no peer review process. The illusion of scientific backing became a commodity anyone could buy.

Cryptocurrency scams promised incredible returns on investments in digital currencies that existed only to steal money from naive investors. "Pump and dump" schemes used social media hype to artificially inflate worthless tokens before the creators sold their holdings and disappeared with the profits.

Fake social media profiles became tools for stalking, harassment, and psychological manipulation. Abusers created multiple accounts to monitor ex-partners, spread false information about enemies, or manufacture evidence of threatening behavior to frame innocent people.

Misinformation campaigns during elections used precision targeting to spread false information about voting procedures, candidate positions, and election results. Voters received personalized lies designed to suppress turnout or manipulate their choices based on detailed psychological profiles built from their online activity.

Deep web markets supported the sale of fake documents, including passports, driver's licenses, and educational credentials. The dark internet became a shopping mall for fraudulent identity documents that looked authentic enough to fool most verification systems.

Live streaming scams used fake emergencies and manufactured crises to generate donations from sympathetic viewers. Streamers claimed their pets needed emergency surgery, their families faced eviction, or they were fleeing domestic violence to extract money from audiences who thought they were helping real people in crisis.

Medical misinformation proliferated through health-focused social media groups where people shared dangerous advice disguised as natural healing wisdom. Alternative medicine communities used emotional testimonials and cherry-picked studies to convince people that mainstream medical treatments were more dangerous than unproven remedies.

Financial fraud schemes used social media to identify and target vulnerable populations with fake investment opportunities. Elderly people became particular targets for scams involving cryptocurrency, precious metals, and get-rich-quick schemes promoted through Facebook ads and email campaigns.

The line between satire and sincere content disappeared as parody accounts and satirical news sites got shared as genuine information. People lost the ability to recognize humor, leading to serious political debates about obviously fictional events and clearly satirical claims.

Synthetic media generation advanced to the point where artificial intelligence could create realistic news articles, social media posts, and even entire websites covering fictional events. The boundary between human-created and machine-generated content became impossible to detect without sophisticated analysis tools.

Corporate disinformation campaigns used the same tactics as foreign propaganda operations to manipulate public opinion about products, environmental issues, and regulatory policies. Oil companies spread climate change denial, tobacco companies minimized health risks, and pharmaceutical companies suppressed negative research using networks of fake experts and manufactured studies.

Insurance fraud moved online as people learned to stage accidents, fake injuries, and fabricate property damage using digital documentation. Social media posts became evidence in fraudulent claims as scammers created entire fictional narratives supported by carefully crafted online histories.

Fake charity scams exploited natural disasters and tragic events to steal donations from people wanting to help. Scammers created websites and social media campaigns for non-existent organizations, using emotional photos and stories to generate sympathy and extract money from compassionate donors.

Diploma mills and fake universities sold worthless degrees and certifications online. People paid thousands of dollars for credentials from institutions that existed only as websites, discovering too late that their "education" was worthless in the real world.

Rental and real estate scams used legitimate property listings to steal deposits from prospective tenants. Scammers copied photos and descriptions from real listings, collected application fees and security deposits, then disappeared, leaving victims without homes or recourse.

Fake tech support operations convinced people their computers were infected with viruses, then charged hundreds of dollars to "fix" non-existent problems. Cold callers claimed to represent

Microsoft or Apple while guiding victims through processes that actually installed malware or stole personal information.

The internet promised to democratize truth by giving everyone access to information. Instead, it democratized lies by giving everyone the tools to create convincing deceptions. We built the ultimate fact-checking machine and used it to manufacture an infinite supply of sophisticated falsehoods.

What Do You Do About This?

Before sharing anything, ask one question: how do you know this is true? Not 'does it seem true' or 'does it feel right' — how do you actually know? Follow the chain to its source. Most viral information traces back to a single article, a single tweet, or a single person who either made it up, misunderstood something, or had a reason to lie. Find that person.

Reverse image search every surprising photo you see online. Right-click, search image, look at where else it appears and when. Photos taken in different countries, different years, or different contexts get repurposed constantly to illustrate stories they have nothing to do with. This takes thirty seconds and will immediately reveal how much visual misinformation circulates in your regular feeds.

Check Snopes, FactCheck.org, and PolitiFact before sharing anything that feels important or outrageous. The major fact-checking organizations have transparent methodologies and correction policies. They are imperfect and still vastly more reliable than your instinct that something feels true.

Phishing attempts have become completely convincing. Emails from your bank, your shipping carrier, your boss — perfectly formatted, using your name, referencing real account details. The only safe rule is never click a link in an email asking you to log in to anything. Go directly to the website. Type the address yourself. This one habit prevents the majority of successful phishing attacks.

Learn what a deepfake looks like, because they're getting harder to spot. Current tells include unnatural blinking, inconsistent lighting around the face and neck, hair that doesn't move quite right, and audio that doesn't perfectly match lip movements. The habit to build now is skepticism toward any video of a public figure saying something surprising, especially close to elections.

Confirmation bias is not a character flaw — it's a cognitive feature that works against you when you're consuming media designed to exploit it. You believe things that confirm what you already believe. The solution isn't to become someone without existing beliefs. It's to apply significantly more scrutiny to information that happens to confirm them.

Misinformation spreads because it's emotionally satisfying. True information is often ambiguous, boring, or unhelpful. False information that validates your worldview feels like evidence. The more something makes you feel vindicated, the more carefully you should check whether it's real.

Call your elderly relatives regularly about scams. Not because they're foolish, but because scam operations specifically target people who grew up when institutions were trustworthy and official-sounding phone calls were credible. The IRS does not call you. Social Security does not suspend your number. The grandparent scam is working every day on people who are not stupid.

Create a family code word for emergency verification. If someone calls claiming to be your child or grandchild in trouble, ask for the code word. Criminals use voice cloning now — they can create convincing audio imitations of family members from a few seconds of public video. The code word verifies human identity in a way that voice alone cannot.

The discomfort of saying 'I don't know if this is true' is much smaller than the embarrassment of having confidently spread false information. Make 'I don't know' your default position on anything you just encountered online. Let verification precede sharing. Always.

Chapter 9: Vanity - The Performance of Self

Social media turned everyone into their own personal brand manager, and most of us are terrible at the job.

The selfie revolution convinced an entire generation that their face was their most valuable asset. People spent hours perfecting the angle, lighting, and expression for a single photo that would be forgotten in minutes. The front-facing camera became a mirror that never stopped reflecting, and we couldn't look away.

The ring light industry exploded as everyone became their own photographer. Professional lighting equipment moved from studios into bedrooms and bathrooms. People invested hundreds of dollars in equipment to make their selfies look more professional, turning their homes into personal photo studios.

Outfit of the day posts turned daily clothing choices into fashion exhibitions. People bought clothes not for comfort or practicality, but for how they would look in photos. Closets became costume departments for daily social media productions. The pressure to never repeat an outfit in photos led to compulsive shopping and debt.

Gym selfies turned fitness into vanity theater. People spent more time photographing their workouts than exercising. Mirror shots with flexed muscles and carefully arranged gym equipment became more important than strength, health, or athletic achievement. The appearance of fitness replaced fitness itself.

Skincare routines became elaborate rituals performed for social media audiences. Ten-step regimens with expensive products got documented and shared as lifestyle content. The effectiveness of the routine mattered less than how sophisticated and expensive it looked to followers.

Personal branding coaches taught ordinary people to market themselves like consumer products. Everyone needed a niche, an aesthetic, and a content strategy. Authentic personality traits got replaced by calculated personas designed to attract followers and engagement. Being genuine became less important than being marketable.

Unboxing videos turned shopping into entertainment. People filmed themselves opening packages and reviewing products, turning consumption into content creation. The excitement of receiving new items became more important than using or enjoying them. Shopping addiction got disguised as product education.

Home staging for social media made living spaces into constantly maintained showrooms. Every corner of every room had to be Instagram-ready at all times. People bought furniture and decorations based on how they would look in photos rather than comfort or functionality. Homes became sets for lifestyle content rather than places to live.

Fake candid photography required elaborate staging to appear spontaneous. "Candid" shots of people laughing, reading, or enjoying nature were carefully orchestrated productions with multiple takes and professional lighting. Authenticity became a performance requiring significant planning and effort.

The golden hour obsession made natural lighting a scheduling priority. People planned their entire days around the brief periods when outdoor lighting was optimal for photography. Activities, meals, and social interactions got timed to coincide with the best natural light for content creation.

Vacation photography turned travel into content production expeditions. People visited destinations primarily for their photogenic potential rather than cultural interest or personal enjoyment. Bucket list locations became backdrops for social media posts rather than places to experience and explore.

The pursuit of the perfect image became more important than enjoying the moment being photographed. People experienced their own lives through the lens of how they would look to others online. Reality became the raw material for social media performance rather than something to be lived and enjoyed directly.

What Do You Do About This?

Stop buying things to photograph. Check your last twenty online purchases and count how many were chosen at least partly because they'd look good on social media. The food at the expensive restaurant, the outfit for the event, the vacation destination that photographs well — you're making real decisions with real money based on how they'll perform for an audience of people who don't care about you.

If you've rearranged your furniture specifically for photos, your home is being optimized for an imaginary audience rather than for the person who actually lives in it. A corner that only exists as a backdrop is not interior design. It's set design for a production nobody asked for.

The filters are making you hate your own face. Dermatologists coined the term 'Snapchat dysmorphia' because patients began requesting cosmetic procedures to look like their filtered versions. The filtered face is not a better version of your face. It's a different face. Getting surgery to match it is not self-improvement. It's self-replacement.

Uninstall TikTok if you're spending more than thirty minutes a day on it. The algorithm is the most sophisticated attention-capture system ever built, and it runs specifically on comparison, aspiration, and performance anxiety. Every video is an implicit benchmark. Every viral creator is an implicit standard. The inadequacy is the product.

Count how many photos you take at the next event you attend where other people are present. Then count how many you actually look back at afterward. For most people, the ratio is embarrassing — hundreds of photos capturing a moment and almost no time spent in it. Document less. Experience more. This is a direct trade-off.

The audience you're performing for doesn't think about you when you're not posting. The people who liked your last post don't think about you. Your followers don't wonder what you're doing today. Your real friends — the ones who actually care about your life — will still know you exist if you don't post for a month. The performance is for an audience that isn't watching between shows.

Delete old posts that make you cringe. Not because they reveal something shameful, but because carrying a public archive of every phase of your self-presentation is a specific kind of psychological weight. You've changed. The posts haven't. You're not obligated to maintain a permanent exhibition of your previous selves.

Your achievements matter whether you post them or not. The job you got, the race you finished, the relationship that's actually good — these things happened and were real before you photographed them. The photograph doesn't validate them. The photograph is not the achievement.

Vanity is ultimately empty. The pursuit of external validation and lifestyle performance leads to anxiety, debt, and dissatisfaction. Real confidence comes from competence, relationships, and internal satisfaction — not from looking good in selfies.

Chapter 10: Tribalism - Digital Division

The internet was supposed to bring humanity together. Instead, it gave us better tools to tear each other apart.

Every platform became a battleground where users sorted themselves into warring tribes based on ideology, identity, and allegiance. The technology designed to connect people across distances ended up dividing people sitting in the same room. Families stopped talking to each other because of what they shared on Facebook.

Sports fandom moved online and became more toxic than ever. Rival team supporters engaged in harassment campaigns that went far beyond trash talk. Social media allowed fans to directly target opposing players, their families, and supporters with death threats and personal attacks. The competitive spirit that used to end when games ended now continued 24/7 online.

Neighborhood social networks like Nextdoor turned suburban communities into surveillance states where residents reported each other for suspicious behavior that usually meant "looking different from me." Local community apps designed to build neighborly cooperation instead encouraged racial profiling, paranoia, and vigilantism.

Academic Twitter became a bloodsport where scholars competed to demonstrate ideological purity through public denunciations of colleagues. University professors destroyed each other's careers over minor disagreements about research methodology or theoretical positions. Higher education became a series of loyalty tests administered through social media platforms.

Parenting philosophy wars raged across mommy blogs and Facebook groups where different approaches to child-rearing became matters of moral superiority. Breastfeeding versus formula, sleep training versus attachment parenting, and vaccination versus natural immunity became tribal identities that determined social allegiances and friendship circles.

Fan communities for movies, books, and television shows split into hostile factions over creative decisions and representation issues. Star Wars fans harassed actors off social media. Harry Potter enthusiasts turned on each other over the author's political statements. Entertainment became another front in the culture wars where artistic preferences became political positions.

Professional industries developed online caste systems where workers sorted themselves by company, role, and career philosophy. Tech workers at different companies engaged in tribal warfare over programming languages, development methodologies, and corporate cultures. Professional networking became professional tribalism.

Dietary communities became religious movements where food choices determined moral worth and social belonging. Vegans, carnivores, keto enthusiasts, and paleo advocates formed separate tribes that viewed other dietary approaches as not just wrong but morally corrupt. Eating became an identity marker that divided people into hostile camps.

Fitness communities fractured into competing philosophies that treated exercise like warfare. CrossFit enthusiasts mocked traditional gym-goers. Runners looked down on weightlifters. Yoga practitioners dismissed high-intensity training. Physical fitness became another way to establish tribal superiority over others.

The internet took every human difference and turned it into a reason for mutual hostility. Instead of creating global community, digital technology created infinite micro-tribes defined by opposition to other micro-tribes. We got connection without understanding, communication without empathy, and community without compassion.

What Do You Do About This?

Stop performing your politics online. Not because your politics are wrong, but because political performance on social media is not politics. It's tribalism cosplaying as engagement. Real political action is unglamorous and unphotographable — it happens in city council meetings, canvassing in neighborhoods, and conversations with people who didn't already agree with you.

When you find yourself categorizing everything — media brands, food companies, clothing, sports teams — by political tribe, the algorithm has gotten into the wiring. Partisan sorting of consumer preferences is a strategy used by media to deepen tribal identity and keep you emotionally invested. You don't need a political opinion about your coffee brand.

Read local news. Find your city or county newspaper and read it weekly. Local governance affects your daily life more concretely than national politics. The tribalism is weaker because local issues are harder to sort into national political teams. It's also where civic engagement produces visible results.

The most effective tactic for breaking out of digital tribalism is extended, genuine conversation with one person you've categorized as the enemy. Not debate — conversation. Not to change their mind — to understand how someone reaches a position you find incomprehensible. One real conversation is more valuable than a thousand social media arguments.

Distinguish between the tribe and the people in it. Online, you encounter the most extreme, most performative members of any group. The actual humans who share broad values with that group are usually nothing like their Twitter representatives. Making judgments about millions of people based on the loudest thousand is how tribalism works. Notice when you're doing it.

Examine which of your tribal loyalties are based on lived experience and which were installed by media. The fear of some out-group, the certainty about some enemy's motivations, the absolute conviction that your side is right about everything — trace those back. Who benefits from your certainty? Who profits from your loyalty?

Sports tribalism is practice for political tribalism. The neural pathways are identical. The emotional responses are identical. The in-group and out-group dynamics are identical. It's not harmful in a sports context. In politics, it produces people who would rather lose with their tribe than win by cooperating with the other side.

When a story makes your side look good and the other side look terrible, apply double skepticism before sharing it. The story that's too perfect, too vindicating, too perfectly illustrative of why your tribe is right — that's the story most likely to be partial, exaggerated, or false.

Facebook's own internal research showed their systems were tearing apart the social fabric and they kept running them anyway because engagement was higher when people were tribal and angry. You didn't arrive at your current level of political outrage by accident. You were led there by a system that profits from your division.

Most people want similar things: safety, prosperity, health, and happiness for themselves and their families. The disagreements are about how to get there — which is real and worth arguing about. The dehumanization is manufactured — which is worth resisting. Keep the argument. Lose the hate.

Chapter 11: Amnesia - The Memory Hole

The internet was supposed to preserve human knowledge forever. Instead, it taught us to forget everything that happened five minutes ago.

We live in an age of infinite information and zero memory. Everything gets documented, but nothing gets remembered. The platforms that promised to create a permanent record of human experience instead created a culture where yesterday's crisis is today's trivia and tomorrow's complete amnesia.

Context collapse turned complex events into isolated incidents with no historical background. People reacted to current events as if they existed in a vacuum, without understanding the years or decades of context that led to those moments. History became irrelevant when every story was treated as breaking news requiring immediate emotional response.

The permanent internet created the paradox of digital amnesia. Everything ever posted online theoretically still exists somewhere, but practically nobody remembers anything that happened more than a week ago. Social media platforms became graveyards of forgotten content that accumulated faster than anyone could process or remember.

Trending topics replaced sustained attention as the dominant form of public discourse. Issues rose to massive public awareness, generated millions of posts and comments, then disappeared completely when algorithm-driven feeds moved on to the next viral content. Problems that required years to solve got abandoned the moment they stopped trending.

The screenshot culture preserved moments out of context while forgetting the circumstances that created them. Old tweets, photos, and posts got weaponized years later without any understanding of when they were created, why they were posted, or what was happening in the world at that time. Digital archaeology became digital persecution.

Search engine optimization destroyed institutional memory by prioritizing recent content over historical accuracy. Websites constantly updated and reorganized their content to appease algorithms, breaking links and losing older information in the process. The internet's own success at finding new content made finding old content nearly impossible.

Social media platforms regularly purged old content, changed their algorithms, or modified their interfaces in ways that made historical posts difficult or impossible to find. Years of conversations, relationships, and experiences disappeared when companies decided old data was less valuable than new engagement metrics.

Link rot destroyed the foundation of internet knowledge as websites disappeared, moved, or changed their content structure. Academic papers, news articles, and reference materials became inaccessible when the URLs pointing to them broke. The web that was supposed to preserve information forever couldn't maintain working links for more than a few years.

Platform migrations erased years of user-generated content when communities moved from one service to another. Forum discussions, photo collections, and social connections disappeared when platforms shut down or users switched to newer services. Digital communities lost their history every time they changed venues.

The algorithmic timeline destroyed chronological memory by presenting information in an order optimized for engagement rather than temporal accuracy. People lost track of when events happened because their feeds jumbled recent and old content together based on what would generate the most clicks rather than what happened when.

Viral content cycles moved so quickly that internet phenomena became historical artifacts within days of their creation. Memes, challenges, and cultural moments that seemed monumentally important at the time of their popularity became completely forgotten a week later. The pace of digital culture made lasting cultural impact nearly impossible.

Subscription fatigue led people to cancel and resubscribe to services repeatedly, losing access to their viewing history, saved content, and personalized recommendations in the process. Digital entertainment became disposable as people forgot what they had watched, read, or listened to on services they no longer subscribed to.

The death of physical media eliminated tangible reminders of cultural products and personal experiences. Digital libraries disappeared when licensing agreements expired or companies went out of business. Movies, books, and music that people had "purchased" digitally became inaccessible when platforms changed their terms or shut down their services.

Password amnesia became epidemic as people relied on browsers and password managers to remember login credentials for hundreds of accounts. When those digital memory aids failed, people lost access to years of emails, photos, documents, and social media history. Digital identity became dependent on technological memory aids that regularly failed.

Cloud storage promised to solve digital amnesia but made it worse by removing the need for people to actively organize and curate their digital possessions. Automatic backups and unlimited storage meant people never had to decide what was worth keeping, leading to vast digital collections that were impossible to navigate or remember.

Version control became version chaos as documents, photos, and files multiplied across different devices, cloud services, and backup systems. People lost track of which version was current, which files were duplicates, and where they had stored important information. Digital organization became digital confusion.

Photo libraries became black holes of forgotten memories as people accumulated thousands of images without ever looking at them again. Automatic photo backups meant every screenshot, accidental shot, and duplicate image got preserved forever while meaningful photos became impossible to find in the digital pile.

Email archives turned into digital graveyards where important messages disappeared among millions of promotional emails, newsletters, and spam. People lost track of important communications because their inboxes became unmanageable repositories of forgotten correspondence.

Bookmark collections became digital hoarding disasters as people saved thousands of links to articles, videos, and websites they never revisited. Browser bookmark lists grew into unnavigable messes where finding previously saved information became harder than searching for it again from scratch.

Digital calendars deleted past events automatically, erasing records of how people had spent their time and who they had met with. Unlike physical calendars that preserved historical records, digital scheduling apps prioritized future events while treating the past as irrelevant data to be discarded.

Social media memories features tried to resurface old content but highlighted random posts based on algorithmic selection rather than personal significance. The platforms decided which memories were worth remembering, often promoting trivial posts while ignoring meaningful moments.

Auto-delete features made forgetting the default option as platforms automatically removed old messages, posts, and files to save storage space. What used to require deliberate effort to forget now happened automatically unless people actively chose to preserve their digital history.

The internet transformed human culture from a system based on institutional memory and accumulated wisdom into a system based on perpetual novelty and constant forgetting. We built the most powerful information preservation system in history and used it to create the most forgetful society that ever existed.

What Do You Do About This?

Before reacting to any current event, spend five minutes finding out what happened five years ago in the same situation. The internet treats everything as unprecedented. Almost nothing is. The pattern repeats. Knowing the pattern gives you actual information instead of manufactured outrage at something that's happened before and will happen again.

Read one history book per year about a period or place you know nothing about. Not pop history — actual history. The value isn't trivia. It's calibration. Understanding how bad things got in real historical crises, and how they resolved or didn't, gives you a baseline for evaluating current events that the internet cannot provide because the internet has no memory.

Context collapse is when a statement made in one context appears in another with the original context stripped out. This is how most outrage moments are generated. Someone says something in a specific conversation, the clip circulates, and thousands of people react to the clip without knowing anything about the conversation. The antidote is asking for context before reacting.

Keep a private record of things you were certain about that turned out to be wrong. Not as self-punishment — as calibration. Most people have no record of their past predictions and therefore no honest accounting of their track record. Your track record on complex current events is probably worse than you think. Knowing that should make you hold positions more lightly.

The permanent record created by the internet is not the same as memory. Screenshots exist, articles survive, but the context around them decays. Something said in 2009 meant something different in 2009 than it means now. Archive without context is not history. It's weaponized amnesia.

Slow down before joining the latest cycle. Ask whether the story generating current outrage will still matter in three months. Most won't. The story dominating your feed right now has a lifespan of approximately 72 hours before the algorithm replaces it with something equally urgent. Save your bandwidth for things that last.

Understand the news cycle as a machine that produces content, not as a system that surfaces important events. Important things happen all the time that receive no coverage. Trivial things become dominant narratives because they generate engagement. What's trending is what the algorithm amplified, not what matters most.

Revisit positions you formed during peak moments. The opinions you formed during maximum outrage — during crises, elections, disasters, scandals — are the least reliable opinions you hold. Go back to them when the temperature has dropped. See if they still hold when you're not in the middle of the emotional event that generated them.

Find one issue you've forgotten about but used to care about. The environmental disaster from two years ago. The humanitarian crisis from eighteen months ago. The corruption case that was going to change everything. Check what actually happened. The gap between peak coverage and silent follow-up is instructive about what the news cycle actually is.

Historical memory is not nostalgia. It's the only context we have for evaluating what's actually happening now. The internet replaced memory with content. Content moves fast and remembers nothing. You are responsible for your own historical context. Nobody else is providing it.

Chapter 12: Apathy - The Illusion of Action

The internet convinced everyone they were changing the world by clicking "like" on social justice posts. Meanwhile, the actual world kept burning while people felt good about their digital activism.

Online petitions became participation theater where people signed digital documents that nobody in power ever read. Change.org collected millions of signatures for causes that never received serious political consideration. The ease of signing online petitions made people feel politically engaged while having zero impact on actual policy decisions.

Awareness campaigns multiplied endlessly without ever moving beyond awareness to action. October was breast cancer awareness month, November was men's health awareness month, December was disability awareness month. Every cause had its awareness ribbon, awareness hashtag, and awareness merchandise. The world became aware of problems without solving any of them.

Viral charity challenges raised money through social media spectacle while participants learned nothing about the causes they supposedly supported. The Ice Bucket Challenge raised funds for ALS research but most participants couldn't explain what ALS was. Charity became performance art where the performance mattered more than the cause.

Click-to-donate schemes promised that engaging with online content would automatically generate charitable donations. Companies pledged to donate money based on likes, shares, and views, turning charity into a marketing strategy that cost donors nothing but made them feel generous. Actual giving decreased as people believed their clicks were sufficient contribution.

Corporate virtue signaling co-opted social movements by turning activist messages into marketing campaigns. Companies changed their logos to rainbow colors during Pride Month while continuing to donate to anti-LGBTQ politicians.

They posted Black Lives Matter statements while maintaining discriminatory hiring practices. Social justice became brand positioning.

The news cycle trained people to care about everything and nothing simultaneously. Every day brought new crises requiring immediate attention and moral outrage. Humanitarian disasters, political scandals, and social injustices competed for limited attention spans. People developed compassion fatigue from the constant demand for emotional response to problems they couldn't address.

Reposting became substitute thinking as people shared articles and videos without reading them or understanding the issues they addressed. The feeling of spreading important information replaced the work of learning about topics deeply enough to have informed opinions or take meaningful action.

Disaster tourism turned tragedies into content opportunities as people rushed to post about earthquakes, shootings, and humanitarian crises they had no connection to. Changing profile pictures to support victims of distant tragedies felt like solidarity while requiring no sacrifice or sustained commitment.

Social media metrics replaced impact measurement as activists focused on likes, shares, and followers rather than policy changes or improved conditions for the people they claimed to help. Success got measured by online engagement rather than real-world outcomes.

Guilt-driven sharing replaced genuine concern as people posted about causes to avoid appearing callous or uninformed. The fear of seeming indifferent to suffering motivated more social media activism than actual care about the issues involved.

Bandwagon activism made supporting popular causes feel obligatory while unpopular or complex issues got ignored. People supported whatever was trending rather than investigating which causes most needed attention or where their efforts could be most effective.

The globalization of outrage meant people spent emotional energy on distant problems they couldn't influence while ignoring local issues where their involvement could make a difference. International crises got more social media attention than neighborhood problems that volunteers could address.

Substitute sympathy replaced genuine empathy as people confused feeling bad about problems with caring enough to solve them. The emotional satisfaction of acknowledging suffering eliminated the motivation to reduce suffering through concrete action.

Digital donations became impulse purchases where people gave small amounts to feel good about themselves rather than making sustained financial commitments to organizations doing effective work. Crowdfunding campaigns raised money for individual sob stories while systematic problems went unfunded.

Crisis fatigue made people numb to genuine emergencies as the constant stream of urgent appeals for attention and money overwhelmed their capacity for sustained concern. When everything was a crisis, nothing felt urgent enough to warrant personal sacrifice or lifestyle changes.

Armchair expertise replaced humble learning as people developed strong opinions about complex global issues based on social media posts and news headlines. The illusion of understanding eliminated curiosity about root causes, historical context, and potential solutions that required more than surface-level engagement.

Virtue hoarding made people collect social causes like fashion accessories, displaying their concern for maximum variety of issues rather than developing deep commitment to specific problems they could meaningfully address.

Slacktivist burnout occurred when people exhausted their capacity for caring through constant exposure to problems they felt powerless to solve. The emotional labor of maintaining concern for dozens of causes simultaneously led to protective apathy and withdrawal from all activism.

Memorial culture turned tragedy into temporary social media observance where people changed profile pictures, posted remembrance messages, and shared moment-of-silence graphics before moving on to the next crisis. Grief became performative rather than transformative.

Cause inflation made every issue seem equally urgent and important, preventing people from prioritizing their limited time, energy, and resources toward problems where their involvement could create meaningful change.

Empathy theater replaced practical compassion as people competed to demonstrate how much they cared about suffering through increasingly dramatic displays of concern that required no sustained effort or personal cost.

Keyboard compassion allowed people to express unlimited sympathy for problems they would never personally address. The ease of posting supportive messages eliminated the social pressure that might have motivated real-world involvement.

Digital activism created the illusion that caring was enough. Feeling bad about injustice became confused with fighting injustice. Emotional response replaced practical action. The internet made it easier than ever to feel like you were changing the world while changing absolutely nothing.

The platforms didn't accidentally create a generation of performative activists. Slacktivism is a feature, not a bug. Engagement that produces no real-world change is the ideal engagement — it captures attention, generates content, and keeps users coming back without ever threatening the systems that generate profit. An informed, organized citizenry taking local action is the one thing the attention economy cannot monetize. Digital activism that goes nowhere is everything it needs.

What Do You Do About This?

Measure your activism by what changed, not by what you expressed. Sign a petition: what legislation passed? Share a hashtag: what policy shifted? Post about awareness month: what did you fund or build? If the answer is nothing, you didn't do activism. You did performance. Performance feels like activism but accomplishes what performance accomplishes — audience attention, briefly.

Stop signing online petitions as a primary form of political engagement. Change.org generated tens of millions in revenue selling advertising to the people who sign their petitions. Politicians receive estimates of authentic constituent engagement behind petition signatures at roughly zero. The petitions generate money for the platform and a feeling of involvement for you. They do not generate legislative pressure.

Pick one local election and actually work on it. Phone bank, knock doors, drive people to polls, stuff envelopes. Presidential politics gets all the glamour and produces nothing you can personally affect. A school board race, a city council seat, a state legislature primary — these are winnable by small numbers of engaged people. You can be one of those people. Show up.

Awareness is not an accomplishment. Every major problem in the world currently has abundant awareness. People are aware of climate change, poverty, systemic racism, and corruption. The awareness did not solve the problems. Solving problems requires resources, sustained effort, organization, and power. None of those come from awareness campaigns. Fund solutions. Build organizations. Vote consistently in non-presidential elections.

If you've ever put a frame on your profile photo for a cause, ask what you did after the frame. If the answer is nothing, the frame was for you. It said something about your values to your social network. It didn't feed anyone, house anyone, change any law, or hold anyone accountable. That's fine. Just know what it was.

Charity should not be content. When you give to causes, the giving is the action. Posting about the giving turns the action into a performance whose primary function is your public image. The two things are not the same.

Long-term local involvement is invisible, unglamorous, and how everything actually changes. Zoning laws, school curricula, local policing policy, public transit, neighborhood development — all of this is shaped by small groups of engaged citizens at interminable public meetings that nobody attends. Show up to one. You will be one of twelve people in a room making decisions about thousands.

Stop sharing fundraisers and cause posts from people you don't know about situations you haven't verified. This behavior generates significant revenue for scammers who craft emotional appeals designed to look like legitimate causes. Before amplifying, verify. Before donating, check the organization at Charity Navigator or GuideStar.

Activism fatigue is real and partially manufactured. The constant churn of causes demanding immediate attention exhausts people into passivity. If everything is urgent, nothing is. Resist the churn by choosing a few causes and staying with them over time. Deep engagement with fewer issues accomplishes more than shallow engagement with everything.

The most effective thing you can do politically is vote in every election, including the ones with bad candidates and low stakes. Down-ballot races determine prosecutors, judges, school boards, and local officials who have more daily impact on your life than federal politicians. Consistency beats intensity.

Chapter 13: Addiction - The Dopamine Trap

Technology companies hired the same psychologists who design casino games to make their products as addictive as possible. They studied operant conditioning, variable reward schedules, and behavioral psychology to create digital experiences that hijack the brain's reward system. Your apps aren't just engaging — they're deliberately engineered to be compulsive.

The infinite scroll eliminated natural stopping points that might allow users to put their devices down. Facebook, Instagram, and TikTok feeds never end because ending would give people a chance to leave. The platforms removed friction from content consumption to make it as frictionless as possible to keep consuming forever.

Streak mechanics borrowed from gaming psychology to create artificial urgency around maintaining daily usage patterns. Snapchat streaks made missing a single day of communication feel like losing weeks of progress. Duolingo guilt-tripped users with sad cartoon owls when they broke learning streaks. Apps manufactured fake consequences for natural breaks in usage.

Red notification badges created visual anxiety that demanded immediate attention. The bright red circles triggered stress responses that made people feel uncomfortable until they cleared all notifications. Apps competed to create the most psychologically irritating notification design because irritation drove engagement.

Autoplay features removed the decision-making friction that might allow users to stop consuming content. YouTube automatically played the next video. Netflix automatically started the next episode. Spotify automatically played similar songs. The platforms eliminated opportunities for users to pause and consider whether they wanted to continue.

Social validation addiction turned likes, comments, and shares into digital drugs that triggered dopamine releases in the brain's reward centers. People refreshed their feeds obsessively checking for new social feedback. The unpredictable timing of social validation created the same addiction patterns as gambling machines.

FOMO algorithms deliberately withheld content to create artificial scarcity and urgency. Instagram stories disappeared after 24 hours. Snapchat messages deleted themselves. Dating apps limited daily matches. The platforms created time pressure and scarcity to make content feel more valuable and urgent than it actually was.

Social media withdrawal created genuine physical and psychological symptoms when users tried to disconnect. People experienced anxiety, depression, phantom vibration syndrome, and compulsive checking behaviors when separated from their devices. Digital detox became necessary medical treatment for technology addiction.

Attention residue made it impossible to focus on non-digital tasks because part of the brain remained fixated on potential notifications and updates. Even when phones were turned off, people experienced intrusive thoughts about messages they might be missing. Digital addiction created cognitive impairment that persisted even during offline activities.

Sleep disruption became endemic as people brought glowing screens into bedrooms and consumed stimulating content before attempting to rest. Blue light exposure suppressed melatonin production while exciting content kept minds racing. Technology addiction destroyed natural sleep cycles and circadian rhythms.

Phantom vibration syndrome made people feel their phones buzzing even when they weren't touching them. The brain's hypervigilance for notifications created false sensory experiences that demonstrated how thoroughly technology had rewired neural pathways. People became so addicted to digital stimulation that they hallucinated it when it wasn't there.

Binge consumption replaced measured media intake as people consumed entire seasons of shows, hours of videos, or endless social media feeds in single sessions. The platforms optimized for marathon usage rather than healthy consumption patterns. Moderation became impossible when the technology was designed to prevent stopping.

Digital hoarding compulsions led people to save thousands of photos, articles, and files they would never revisit. The unlimited storage available through cloud services enabled information hoarding that created anxiety about missing or losing digital possessions. People developed emotional attachments to digital clutter.

Multitasking addiction made people feel uncomfortable doing only one thing at a time. Constant digital stimulation created expectations for perpetual input that made focused attention feel boring and insufficient. People lost the ability to be present in single activities without additional digital stimulation.

Comparison addiction turned social media into an endless cycle of measuring personal worth against others' curated presentations. People became addicted to checking how their lives measured up to friends, influencers, and strangers. Social comparison became a compulsive behavior that consistently decreased happiness and self-esteem.

App switching compulsion made people cycle through the same applications repeatedly even when they had already checked them minutes earlier. Users developed muscle memory patterns of opening Facebook, then Instagram, then Twitter, then starting the cycle again without conscious awareness of their behavior.

Refresh addiction created compulsive pull-to-refresh behaviors where people repeatedly updated feeds hoping for new content. The physical motion of pulling down to refresh became a nervous habit that people performed hundreds of times per day even when they knew no new content was available.

Screen time anxiety developed as people became aware of their excessive device usage but felt powerless to reduce it. Weekly screen time reports created shame and guilt without providing effective tools for behavior change. Awareness of the problem became another source of stress rather than motivation for improvement.

Digital productivity addiction made people obsessed with optimization, tracking, and measurement rather than actual accomplishment. Users spent more time configuring productivity systems than being productive. The pursuit of the perfect productivity setup became procrastination disguised as self-improvement.

Upgrade addiction created compulsive desires for new devices, apps, and features that promised to solve problems the current technology couldn't address. People became convinced that the next phone, the next app update, or the next digital tool would finally provide the satisfaction that previous upgrades had failed to deliver.

Variable ratio reward schedules in social media created the strongest possible addiction patterns by making positive feedback unpredictable and random. Users never knew when their next post would receive likes or comments, creating the same psychological dependency that keeps gamblers pulling slot machine levers.

The addiction economy grew into a trillion-dollar industry built on exploiting human psychological vulnerabilities for profit. Technology companies measured success by time-on-device and user engagement rather than user wellbeing. The business model required addiction to function profitably.

We handed our brains to companies whose entire business model depends on making us compulsively use their products. They succeeded beyond their wildest dreams, creating a generation of people who can't put their phones down, can't focus on single tasks, and can't be alone with their thoughts. The devices meant to enhance human capability instead made us dependent, distracted, and addicted.

What Do You Do About This?

Look at your screen time report right now. The average American spends four hours a day on their phone. Whatever your number is, multiply it across seven years and think about how many weeks of your life that amounts to. The number will be uncomfortable. That's the point.

The variable reward schedule — sometimes you get likes, sometimes you don't, sometimes the scroll delivers something great, usually it doesn't — is the same mechanism that makes slot machines addictive. This is not a metaphor. The engineers who designed these systems studied slot machine psychology. You're playing a slot machine that costs attention instead of money.

Delete the social apps from your phone. Not the accounts — the apps. You can still access Instagram through a browser on your computer. The browser version is slower, less gamified, and not specifically optimized to maximize time-on-platform. The friction makes a measurable difference. Most people who do this find their daily use drops by 60-70% in the first week.

Charge your phone in a room you don't sleep in. The phone in the bedroom creates an immediate morning and late-night access point for the dopamine loop. Most people check their phone within two minutes of waking up and within thirty minutes of trying to sleep. Both behaviors consistently degrade sleep quality and morning cognitive function. This one physical change reliably alters usage patterns.

Turn off all push notifications except calls and text messages from specific contacts. Every other notification is an interruption engineered to pull you back into the app. App companies measure success in daily active users and time-on-platform. Notifications are their recruitment mechanism. Every time you respond to one, you've been successfully recruited.

The streak mechanic is deliberate manipulation. Snapchat, Duolingo, fitness apps — they all use streaks because losing a streak feels like losing something you own. You don't own it. The platform owns it. The only thing the streak does is make breaking the habit feel like a loss rather than a choice. Name this. Then make the choice when you need to.

Boredom is not a problem to be solved with your phone. Boredom is a cognitive state where your brain consolidates memory, generates creative connections, and resets its attention capacity. Eliminating all boredom via constant phone use means eliminating those functions. Your brain needs unstructured time. Stop filling every gap with content.

Talk to your doctor if you've tried and failed repeatedly to control your social media or smartphone use. This is not a willpower problem requiring more effort. The technology was engineered by teams of behavioral scientists to be specifically difficult to stop using. There are behavioral approaches and, in some cases, clinical interventions that treat technology addiction as the addiction it is.

One-week digital sabbaticals are more effective than daily usage limits. The apps are too good at making you forget you're trying to limit them. A full week away breaks the automatic behavioral loop entirely. It's uncomfortable for the first two days, neutral by day four, and clarifying by day seven. Most people who do this report that the pull back to the apps is significantly weaker afterward.

The companies profiting from your addiction are not going to fix it. The U.S. Surgeon General issued warnings about social media and adolescent mental health. The platforms made incremental, performative adjustments and kept the core engagement mechanics intact. Regulation is coming slowly. Your brain is being used now. Treat it accordingly.

Chapter 14: Children - The Intended Targets

Every manipulation tactic described in this book was designed with children in mind. Not because tech companies are unusually evil, but because children are the most profitable users across platforms. They have fewer defenses, more malleable habits, and a lifetime of engagement ahead of them. The addiction mechanics, the comparison triggers, the infinite scroll — all of it works better on a developing brain than on an adult one. That's not a coincidence. That's optimization.

The average age of first smartphone ownership is eleven by some estimates. The average age of first social media account is twelve, though many children create accounts earlier using false birthdates that platforms don't verify because verification would reduce user counts. The average age of first pornography exposure is eleven. By the time most children reach high school, they have spent years being trained by systems built by adults who understood exactly what they were doing to developing brains.

Social media rewires the adolescent brain during the precise developmental window when identity, self-worth, and social comparison are most intensely felt. The teenage brain is neurologically primed to care about peer judgment — it's how human social development works. Instagram and TikTok didn't create adolescent insecurity. They industrialized it, quantified it with like counts and follower numbers, and made it available twenty-four hours a day with no off switch.

Teen girls have been the most thoroughly documented casualties. The internal Facebook research leaked by Frances Haugen showed that Instagram's own data scientists found the platform made body image issues worse for one in three teenage girls, increased rates of anxiety and depression, and that teens who reported suicidal ideation traced the ideation to Instagram use. The company knew. The platform ran unchanged. The engagement numbers were too good.

Teen boys face different but equally documented harms. Algorithm-driven radicalization pipelines have been extensively studied — the progression from gaming content to masculinity content to increasingly extreme political content is a documented phenomenon, not a theory. Boys who would never seek out extremist material get guided there incrementally by recommendation engines that optimize for watch time. The content that performs best on the path is content that validates grievance and provides simple enemies.

The education system has been colonized by screens without meaningful evidence that screens improve educational outcomes. Tablet programs were sold to school districts with marketing budgets, not research. Laptops in classrooms increase distraction and decrease retention on standardized measures. The major tech companies donated equipment, lobbied for digital curriculum mandates, and shaped policy in their favor while the research on learning outcomes remained mixed at best. Children got less practice with sustained reading, handwriting, and the kind of focused attention that academic work requires.

Child influencers represent perhaps the most visible exploitation — children turned into content generators by parents who collect the revenue while the children work. But the more pervasive exploitation is subtler: every child with a social media account is being trained to perform their life for an audience, to measure their worth in engagement metrics, and to understand their relationships as content. This is not a neutral technological development. It is a wholesale reorientation of childhood toward production and consumption at the expense of play, privacy, and unmonitored development.

The research on screen time and children's mental health has become one of the most replicated findings in contemporary psychology. Increased screen time correlates with increased anxiety, increased depression, decreased sleep quality, decreased in-person social skills, and decreased attention span. The correlations are consistent across dozens of studies in multiple countries. The tech industry disputes the causation while the correlations pile up. The disputed causation is their legal and regulatory strategy, not a genuine scientific position.

Parents are largely on their own. Platform age verification is theatrical. Content moderation for minors is inadequate. The regulatory frameworks governing what companies can do to children online were written before anyone understood what these platforms were capable of. The Children's Online Privacy Protection Act covers children under thirteen. It does nothing for the thirteen-year-old on Instagram for eight hours a day. The gap between the law and the reality of children's digital lives is where the damage accumulates.

This is the generation that will govern, innovate, and inherit whatever remains of human institutions. They are being raised by systems that profit from their distraction, their insecurity, and their inability to concentrate for longer than thirty seconds. The adults who designed those systems are sending their own children to screen-free schools. That gap — between what the tech industry builds for other people's children and what it provides for its own — is the most honest assessment of the damage available.

What Do You Do About This?

No phones until high school. This is the recommendation of most child psychologists who have studied the research, the policy position Jonathan Haidt has argued extensively with supporting data, and the practice of parents who work in tech. The pushback will be that your child is the only one without a phone. The pushback is usually wrong, and even when it's right, it's not a sufficient reason.

If your child has a smartphone, put it on the charger outside their bedroom at nine PM. Sleep deprivation from late-night phone use is documented in adolescents at epidemic levels. Sleep is when the adolescent brain consolidates learning, regulates emotion, and builds the executive function that manages impulse control. The phone in the bedroom is competing with brain development. There is no social need that requires a thirteen-year-old to be reachable at midnight.

Know what your child is actually watching on YouTube and TikTok. Not occasionally — regularly. The recommendation algorithms show children content that an adult would recognize as problematic within minutes of watching it. Children often don't. The progression from benign to harmful happens gradually enough that children don't notice the trajectory. Watching with them occasionally is the only way to see what the algorithm is doing.

Talk to your child's school about phone policies before there's a problem. Schools with phone-free policies — phones collected at the start of the day, returned at dismissal — report measurable improvements in social interaction, focus, and reported wellbeing. The research supports this. The opposition is mostly from parents who want to be able to reach their children during school hours. A school phone for emergencies solves that problem. Phones in classrooms don't solve any educational problem.

Age verification is a political issue, not a technical one. The technology to implement real age verification exists. The platforms choose not to implement it because it would reduce user counts. Support politicians and legislation that mandate age verification with enforcement mechanisms. The tobacco industry didn't stop marketing to children voluntarily. The social media industry won't either.

If your child is struggling with anxiety, depression, or social difficulties, their therapist should specifically ask about social media use, gaming habits, and screen time patterns. Many therapists don't ask. You should raise it. The research on the relationship between social media use and adolescent mental health is strong enough that any clinical picture of an adolescent is incomplete without it.

The family code word works for children too — not just for scam prevention, but as a general principle: create easy off-ramps from uncomfortable situations. A child who has a pre-arranged signal to get a parent to come pick them up without having to explain why is a child who will use that option. Remove the social cost of asking for help.

Talk to your children about what the platforms are actually doing. Not to frighten them — to arm them. They're old enough to understand that the like count is engineered to make them feel bad about themselves. They're old enough to understand that the algorithm is optimizing for their engagement, not their wellbeing. Knowing the mechanism doesn't make them immune, but it gives them language for what they're experiencing and a framework for pushing back.

The hardest thing about protecting children from digital harm is that it requires going against the current. Other children have phones. Other parents don't restrict screen time. The path of least resistance leads directly into the platforms. Choosing otherwise means accepting that your child will be different from their peers, at least temporarily, and managing the friction that creates. That friction is the cost of the protection. It's worth paying.

Chapter 15: Commodification - Everything for Sale

The internet turned human relationships into content, personal trauma into entertainment, and basic human dignity into a business opportunity.

Family vloggers transformed childhood into a performance where children became unpaid actors in their parents' content creation business. Kids who couldn't consent to having their entire lives documented and monetized grew up as products in the family entertainment industry. Parents filmed their children's tantrums, potty training, and private moments to generate revenue from strangers watching their family dysfunction.

Tragedy profiteering turned personal disasters into fundraising opportunities where people monetized their suffering for social media audiences. Cancer diagnoses became content series. House fires became GoFundMe campaigns. Family deaths became viral charity drives. The line between genuine need and exploitation disappeared when personal catastrophe became a revenue stream.

Grief tourism emerged as people traveled to disaster sites and tragedy locations to create content about other people's suffering. Influencers posed for photos at memorial sites, used natural disasters as backdrops for lifestyle content, and turned humanitarian crises into opportunities for virtue signaling and audience growth.

Poverty porn made entertainment out of economic hardship as content creators exploited homeless people, struggling families, and desperate situations for views and donations. Homeless makeover videos, surprise bill payments, and charity stunts turned human desperation into feel-good content that made viewers feel charitable while treating poor people as props.

Mental health monetization turned therapy sessions, medication trials, and psychological breakdowns into shareable content. People documented their depression, anxiety, and trauma recovery journeys for audience engagement. Personal healing became performance art where recovery was less important than maintaining subscriber interest in the mental health struggle.

Relationship commodification made romantic partnerships into content creation collaborations where couples documented their entire romantic lives for public consumption. Proposals, anniversaries, fights, and breakups became monetized content. Love became a business partnership where personal intimacy was the product being sold to audiences.

Pregnancy and birth became content franchises where people documented conception attempts, pregnancy symptoms, labor, and early parenthood as entertainment series. The most intimate and vulnerable human experiences got packaged as lifestyle content for strangers to consume wholesale.

Therapy culture made psychological concepts into social media trends where complex mental health terms became casual content categories. Trauma bonding, gaslighting, and narcissistic abuse became hashtags and viral explanations for relationship problems that reduced psychological complexity to shareable oversimplifications.

Disability exploitation turned physical and cognitive differences into inspiration porn where disabled people became motivational content for able-bodied audiences. Disabled people got reduced to their conditions and expected to perform inspiration and gratitude for others' entertainment and emotional satisfaction.

Child labor laws didn't apply to social media where parents could force their children to work unlimited hours creating content without wages, workplace protections, or educational guarantees. Child influencers became the new child actors in an industry with no oversight or safeguards.

We built an economy where human vulnerability became the most valuable commodity and personal suffering became the most engaging content. The platforms that promised to connect us instead taught us to extract value from our most intimate experiences and package our pain for public consumption.

What Do You Do About This?

If you're posting your children online with any regularity, your children did not consent to that. Not the cute videos, not the milestone posts, not the funny moments. The child who appears in those videos will be an adult someday, looking at footage of themselves that strangers watched and commented on during their childhood. Several family vloggers' children have already reached adulthood and are explicitly describing harm. Listen to them.

The family vlogger industry generates revenue by turning children into unpaid performers in content they didn't choose. The parents earn. The children don't. The exposure is permanent. This is not hypothetical future harm. It is documented present harm.

Your personal trauma is yours. You can share it if you choose. What you should consider is whether the audience witnessing your grief, your addiction recovery, or your mental health crisis is actually serving you or serving the platform's engagement metrics. Healing and performing healing are different processes. Many therapists note that public performance of healing often substitutes for the actual work.

Grief content specifically is a category that should not exist. Videos of people crying about dead loved ones, accumulated into channels with millions of subscribers, represent something new and troubling — grief turned into entertainment, the bereaved monetizing their most private moments for an audience that experiences their pain as compelling content.

The hustle culture that turned every hobby into a side hustle and every interest into a brand has stripped pleasure out of a generation's leisure time. Baking is not a business. Photography is not a brand. Playing guitar is not content creation. When you monetize a passion, you change your relationship to it permanently. The enjoyment becomes evaluation. The play becomes performance.

If you've filmed someone else's worst moment — an accident, a crisis, a breakdown — for social media, that is a choice with a clear victim. The viral video of someone having a mental health crisis is entertainment for its audience and a permanent humiliation for the subject. Put down the camera.

Authenticity marketing — the strategy of selling access to your 'real' life — is still marketing. The 'authentic' influencer showing you their messy house and real struggles is doing it because it converts better than polished content. The mess is selected. The vulnerability is curated. The authenticity is a product.

When platforms pay creators for content about mental illness, addiction, eating disorders, and trauma, they create financial incentives for people to produce that content regardless of whether producing it is good for them. The creator economy monetizes suffering. Understand the economic structure behind the content before you engage with it.

Children's privacy should not be traded for engagement. Not for charities. Not for awareness campaigns. Not even for genuinely good causes. A parent who posts their child's medical diagnosis for fundraising is making a choice the child cannot make about permanent public disclosure of sensitive personal information.

Decide what parts of your life are not for sale and hold that line. Your children's childhoods. Your grief. Your healing. Your intimate relationships. These things have value precisely because they aren't products. Commodifying them doesn't make them more valuable. It makes them less yours.

Chapter 16: The Metaverse - Escaping Reality Into Digital Nowhere

Technology companies decided that real life wasn't engaging enough, so they're building virtual worlds where people can live entire lives without ever having to deal with physical reality.

Virtual real estate speculation created markets for digital land that cost real money but existed only as server space. People spent thousands of dollars buying plots in virtual worlds that could disappear forever if the companies hosting them went bankrupt or lost interest.

Avatar identity disorder allowed people to become whoever they wanted in virtual spaces, leading to psychological confusion about authentic identity versus digital persona. The gap between virtual appearance and physical reality created new forms of body dysmorphia and self-hatred.

Digital workplace colonization moved employment into virtual offices where employees worked as avatars in simulated environments. Companies discovered they could save money on physical space while monitoring employee behavior more completely in digital environments.

Virtual event replacement substituted digital gatherings for physical meetings, concerts, and social interactions. The shared experience of being physically present with other humans got replaced by networked isolation disguised as connection.

Metaverse addiction created compulsive use patterns where people preferred virtual experiences to physical activities. The carefully designed engagement mechanics of virtual worlds made digital life more satisfying than real life for people seeking achievement and social connection.

Digital goods consumption encouraged spending real money on virtual items that had no physical existence. People bought clothes for avatars, decorations for virtual homes, and status symbols that existed only as computer code.

Virtual relationship substitution replaced human connections with interactions between avatars that could be anonymous, deceptive, or entirely artificial. Romance, friendship, and family relationships moved into digital spaces where authenticity became impossible to verify.

Sensory replacement technology promised to make virtual experiences feel physically real through haptic feedback, virtual reality headsets, and brain-computer interfaces that could eventually replace physical sensation with digital simulation.

Economic virtual worlds created entirely digital economies where people could earn virtual currency by performing virtual labor for virtual rewards. The gamification of work made exploitation feel like entertainment.

Metaverse surveillance enabled unprecedented monitoring of user behavior, conversations, and activities in virtual environments where every action got logged and analyzed. Privacy disappeared completely in digital worlds where companies controlled every interaction.

Virtual property rights created legal confusion about ownership of digital assets, virtual creations, and avatar identities that existed only within corporate-controlled platforms that could change or eliminate them without notice.

Reality displacement occurred as virtual worlds became more visually impressive and socially rewarding than physical life. People began spending more time in digital environments than in the real world where their physical bodies existed.

Virtual world platform dependence made users completely reliant on technology companies for access to their digital lives, social connections, and virtual possessions. Corporate control over virtual worlds exceeded any historical precedent for private power over human social interaction.

Avatar harassment created new forms of sexual assault, stalking, and violence that occurred in virtual environments but caused real psychological trauma to users whose avatars experienced simulated attacks.

Virtual world collapse risks threatened to destroy years of user investment when companies shut down metaverse platforms, changed business models, or lost interest in maintaining virtual worlds that users had built their digital lives around.

Physical world neglect became epidemic as people invested more time, energy, and resources in virtual achievements than in maintaining their physical health, real relationships, and actual living environments.

Metaverse child exploitation created new venues for predators to access and groom minors through virtual interactions that felt like games but provided opportunities for abuse that were difficult for parents and authorities to monitor.

Digital world manipulation allowed companies to alter virtual environments, modify user experiences, and control social interactions in ways that influenced behavior, spending, and political beliefs without users realizing they were being manipulated.

Virtual currency speculation created volatile markets for digital tokens that had value only within specific virtual worlds, leading to financial losses when virtual economies collapsed or companies changed their policies.

The metaverse promised to expand human experience by creating unlimited virtual worlds, but delivered sophisticated escapism that encouraged people to abandon physical reality rather than improve it.

What Do You Do About This?

Mark Zuckerberg spent $36 billion building a virtual world that the public refused to inhabit. The metaverse, as of this writing, is populated by a handful of corporate meeting avatars and early adopters. This is instructive. The tech industry consistently projects its own enthusiasm onto the general public and consistently discovers that people prefer physical reality when they have access to it.

Virtual real estate has no floor. When the platform disappears, the asset goes with it. Decentraland, The Sandbox, and similar blockchain-based virtual worlds sold millions of dollars in virtual land to investors now holding assets worth a fraction of what they paid. This is not like buying land in a bad neighborhood. This is buying land in a neighborhood that might not exist next year.

The case for VR as the future of social interaction has been made for thirty years. Every five years the technology improves and the adoption curve disappoints. Real people in physical proximity generate experiences that headset avatars do not replicate — touch, spatial presence, pheromones, the thousand nonverbal cues that constitute actual human interaction. VR will keep getting better. It will not become a substitute for being somewhere.

The metaverse pitch exploits real loneliness. People who are isolated, underemployed, or geographically stuck found genuine community in online games and virtual worlds. That's real. The corporations that packaged those genuine human needs into investment vehicles and NFT schemes were parasitically extracting from real human pain. The community is sometimes real. The financial opportunity almost never is.

Avatar identity — the gap between who you are in virtual space and who you are physically — is not inherently harmful. The harm comes from using the virtual self as a substitute for developing the physical self. If you prefer your avatar's life to your actual life in ways that prevent you from improving your actual life, that's a problem worth naming.

Children in virtual worlds need active supervision, not just content filters. The metaverse and its predecessors — Roblox, Minecraft servers, Second Life — have documented histories of adult predators using platform features to access children. Content filters don't catch social engineering. A predator doesn't need to show your child anything inappropriate. They need to build a relationship first.

The technology industry is selling you presence in virtual worlds as a solution to the isolation and disconnection that their technology helped create. Social media eroded physical community. Now the next product cycle sells you a virtual community as the solution. The illness and the medicine are sold by the same company.

Platform risk in virtual worlds is total. If Meta shuts down Horizon Worlds, every relationship, achievement, and investment inside it disappears. Your local coffee shop closes and you lose a gathering place. Your virtual world closes and you lose everything inside it, including people you may have only known there.

The most powerful technology for human connection invented in the last fifty years is the reliable video call. Not VR. Not social media. A video call with someone you actually know, in which you can see their face clearly and hear their voice, is more connective than any avatar interaction currently possible. Use what actually works.

Physical reality is inconvenient, messy, and difficult. It's also the place where everything that matters actually happens. Relationships, work, health, community, purpose — all of it exists in physical space. The metaverse offers escape from reality's inconveniences. It cannot offer the rewards that only reality produces.

Chapter 17: Artificial Intelligence - The Automation of Everything

Artificial intelligence promised to augment human intelligence and creativity. Instead, it's replacing human judgment with algorithmic decision-making that nobody understands or controls.

Machine learning hiring systems automated employment decisions using criteria that screened out qualified candidates based on hidden biases while missing the intangible qualities that make employees valuable beyond their resume qualifications.

Predictive policing algorithms guided law enforcement decisions about where to patrol and whom to investigate based on historical crime data that reflected existing police bias, creating feedback loops that intensified discrimination in criminal justice.

Credit scoring automation replaced human loan officers with algorithms that made lending decisions based on data patterns that often discriminated against minority applicants while claiming mathematical objectivity.

Medical diagnosis AI made healthcare decisions based on pattern recognition that couldn't account for unusual cases, patient preferences, or the intuitive judgment that experienced physicians develop through years of practice.

Facial recognition surveillance automated monitoring and control by recognizing faces and analyzing behavior patterns using criteria that reflected the biases and assumptions of their programmers rather than objective threats.

Content moderation AI replaced human judgment about appropriate online content with automated systems that couldn't understand context, satire, or cultural differences, leading to arbitrary censorship and inconsistent enforcement.

Autonomous weapons development created killing machines that could select and engage targets without human oversight, removing human judgment from decisions about when to use lethal force in military conflicts.

Financial trading algorithms created markets dominated by automated transactions that moved faster than human comprehension, causing flash crashes and market instability when AI systems made decisions based on flawed data.

Educational AI assessment systems evaluated student performance and determined academic opportunities using standardized metrics that couldn't account for learning differences, creativity, or non-traditional forms of intelligence.

Customer service chatbots replaced human representatives with systems that couldn't understand complex problems, show empathy, or make exceptions to policies when circumstances required human judgment and flexibility.

AI content generation flooded the internet with synthetic articles, images, and videos that looked authentic but were created by machines optimizing for virality rather than truth or artistic value.

Deepfake technology created synthetic media that made it impossible to distinguish between authentic and fabricated video evidence, undermining trust in visual documentation and enabling unprecedented propaganda campaigns.

Personal AI assistants collected intimate data about users' daily lives while providing services that made people dependent on algorithmic management of their schedules, decisions, and relationships.

Recommendation algorithms controlled what people saw, bought, and believed by optimizing for engagement rather than truth, accuracy, or human wellbeing, shaping culture and politics while pursuing goals unrelated to social benefit.

Insurance AI pricing used personal data and behavioral patterns to calculate individualized rates that could discriminate against people based on factors they couldn't control while claiming actuarial objectivity.

Language translation AI eliminated the need for human translators while missing cultural nuances, emotional undertones, and contextual meanings that made communication more than literal word conversion.

Resume screening automation rejected job applicants based on algorithmic analysis that favored certain educational backgrounds, career paths, and demographic characteristics while missing qualified candidates with non-traditional experiences.

News curation algorithms determined what information people received about current events by optimizing for engagement metrics that favored sensational and divisive content over accurate and important reporting.

Legal research AI automated law practice by analyzing contracts and predicting case outcomes, reducing legal work to algorithmic pattern matching that missed nuanced human factors in complex disputes.

Voice recognition systems failed to understand accents, dialects, and speech patterns that differed from their training data, creating barriers for non-native speakers and people with speech differences.

The AI revolution automated human intelligence without understanding what intelligence actually is, creating systems that could mimic human performance without possessing human wisdom, empathy, or judgment.

What Do You Do About This?

Demand to know when a consequential decision about you is being made by an algorithm. Your mortgage application. Your job application. Your insurance rate. Your bail determination. In many cases, you have a legal right to this information and a right to request human review. Exercise these rights.

Algorithms making these decisions are frequently wrong in systematic ways that correlate with race, gender, and income.

AI-generated text is now pervasive enough that you can't reliably detect it by feel. This matters when you're reading medical information, legal information, financial advice, or news. AI systems generate confident, fluent text regardless of whether the information is accurate. Verify medical and legal information through licensed professionals, not through systems that hallucinate with perfect grammar.

Learn one skill that AI cannot currently replicate and become genuinely good at it. Physical skills, genuine interpersonal skills, creative judgment, domain expertise developed over years — these are things that AI augments rather than replaces at the moment. Be good at something real.

Companies deploying AI in hiring, lending, and criminal justice claim their systems are objective because they don't use race as an explicit variable. What they use are proxy variables — zip codes, school names, linguistic patterns — so correlated with race that the discrimination is functionally identical. Claiming objectivity because the prejudice is laundered through data doesn't make it objective.

Copyright law has not caught up to AI training. The models generating images, text, and music were trained on copyrighted material without compensation to creators. This is not settled law and not settled ethics. If you're using AI-generated content commercially, understand that the legal ground is unstable and the ethical ground is contested.

The AI productivity tools being sold to businesses will increase output per worker, and employers will reduce headcount accordingly. This is the historical pattern with every automation technology. The output gains are real. The distribution of those gains consistently skews toward owners and away from workers. Advocate for policies that distribute the gains.

Be specific about what AI is actually doing well versus what it's being deployed for before it's ready. AI is excellent at certain narrow tasks and unreliable at others. Medical diagnosis from images — often excellent. Medical advice from text — often dangerous. Know the difference and apply appropriate skepticism accordingly.

The AI making decisions about your life is owned by someone with interests. Those interests are not identical to yours. The AI your health insurer uses to evaluate your claims is optimized to minimize payouts. The AI your employer uses to evaluate your productivity is optimized to find reasons for corrective action. Understand whose interests the system serves before trusting its outputs about you.

Support legislation requiring algorithmic auditing with teeth — not voluntary transparency reports, but mandatory third-party audits of AI systems making consequential decisions, with enforcement mechanisms for discriminatory outcomes. This exists in limited form in the EU. It does not meaningfully exist in the US. Vote for the people who will build it.

The most important thing to understand about AI right now is that it's being deployed by people who profit from its deployment into situations where its failure modes are not fully understood. The pace of deployment exceeds the pace of safety research. You are in a real-world experiment. Knowing that is the beginning of navigating it intelligently.

If your employer is deploying AI to monitor your productivity, your communications, or your work patterns, find out specifically what it measures and how those measurements affect your employment. This is not paranoia — employee monitoring AI is standard in large companies now. The outputs feed performance reviews, raise decisions, and termination recommendations. You have a right to know what data is being collected about you and how it's being used.

AI systems trained primarily on English-language data from Western sources produce outputs that reflect those biases. When AI translates, summarizes, or analyzes content about non-Western cultures, communities, or contexts, treat the outputs with extra skepticism. The training data determines the worldview. Most major AI systems were built from a narrow slice of human experience.

Creative workers — writers, designers, artists, musicians — are navigating a genuine threat to their livelihoods that most AI discourse dismisses as technophobia. The economic harm is real and documented. If you use AI-generated creative work commercially, understand that the cost savings come at someone's expense. Support human creators directly. Buy the book, the album, the commission.

The AI tools being sold as productivity solutions often create new work while eliminating old work. Reviewing AI outputs for errors, hallucinations, and bias takes time. Prompting effectively takes skill. Maintaining oversight of AI decisions takes attention. The efficiency gains are real in some contexts and illusory in others. Measure actual time saved before committing workflows to AI dependency.

AI safety research is roughly a decade behind AI deployment. The systems being integrated into hiring, medicine, criminal justice, and financial markets were built and deployed faster than anyone could evaluate their failure modes. This isn't a reason for panic — it's a reason to maintain human oversight of consequential decisions for longer than feels necessary. The cost of a wrong call by a human is recoverable. The cost of a systematic wrong call by an AI at scale is not.

Chapter 18: Digital Divide - The New Inequality

The internet promised to democratize information and opportunity. Instead, it created new forms of inequality that made traditional class divisions look quaint by comparison.

Broadband access became the new postal service, except the government didn't guarantee universal delivery. Rural communities, poor neighborhoods, and developing regions got left behind in the digital revolution while wealthy areas enjoyed high-speed connections that enabled economic opportunities unavailable to the disconnected.

Device inequality separated society into smartphone classes where the quality of your technology determined your access to jobs, education, and essential services. People with outdated phones couldn't use apps required for employment, banking, or government services, creating a technological caste system.

Digital literacy requirements excluded millions of people from basic participation in modern society. Job applications, healthcare enrollment, government benefits, and educational opportunities moved online while assuming everyone possessed computer skills that many people never had the chance to develop.

Age-based digital discrimination created generational technology gaps that left older adults unable to access services increasingly available only through digital platforms. Seniors became second-class citizens in a society that assumed everyone could navigate smartphone apps and websites.

Educational technology inequality provided wealthy schools with advanced computers, high-speed internet, and digital learning tools while poor schools struggled with outdated equipment and unreliable connections. The homework gap meant students without home internet access fell further behind academically.

Healthcare digitization moved medical services online through telemedicine platforms that required high-speed internet, modern devices, and digital literacy skills. Patients without technological access lost access to medical care during emergencies and routine treatment.

Financial technology exclusion locked millions of people out of digital banking, online payments, and economic opportunities available only through smartphone apps and internet platforms. The unbanked became the digitally excluded.

Language barriers multiplied online where most content and services were available only in dominant languages. Non-English speakers faced additional obstacles to accessing information, services, and opportunities in digital spaces designed for linguistic majorities.

Geographic discrimination concentrated technology infrastructure in profitable urban and suburban areas while leaving rural and remote communities with inadequate internet service that limited their economic development and educational opportunities.

Disability access failures made most digital platforms unusable for people with visual, hearing, mobility, or cognitive impairments. The internet became less accessible than physical spaces that were required to accommodate disabilities.

Economic digital barriers required upfront costs for devices, monthly service fees, and ongoing upgrade expenses that low-income families couldn't afford. The cost of staying connected became another monthly expense that separated economic classes.

Technical support inequality meant wealthy users could afford professional help with technology problems while poor users had to rely on inadequate customer service or remain locked out of digital services when technical issues arose.

Digital document requirements forced people to own printers, scanners, and other equipment to participate in employment, education, and government services. Basic civic participation required expensive technology ownership.

Data cost discrimination made internet access proportionally more expensive for low-income users who couldn't afford unlimited data plans or high-speed service. Poor people paid more per gigabyte for inferior internet access.

Government service digitization moved essential services online without providing alternative access methods for people who couldn't use digital platforms. Applying for benefits, paying taxes, and accessing government services required internet access and computer skills.

Social capital digital gaps meant that people without technology access lost connections to job networks, educational opportunities, and social support systems that increasingly operated through digital platforms and social media.

Emergency service digitization created life-threatening situations for people without smartphones or internet access when disaster alerts, evacuation notices, and emergency communications moved to digital-only formats.

Digital banking requirements eliminated cash-based transactions and check-cashing services that low-income people depended on, forcing them into expensive alternative financial services or complete exclusion from economic participation.

Gig economy exclusion prevented people without smartphones, reliable internet, or bank accounts from participating in ride-sharing, food delivery, and other app-based employment that provided economic opportunities for digitally connected workers.

Telehealth expansion created two-tier medical care where wealthy patients accessed convenient virtual consultations while poor patients lost access to healthcare when in-person services moved online without providing technology access.

The digital divide doesn't look like inequality because it's invisible from the connected side. If you have reliable broadband, a current device, and the digital literacy to navigate government websites, healthcare portals, and job applications, the divide isn't your daily reality — it's an abstract problem you read about. That invisibility is why it persists. The people making infrastructure decisions, writing technology policy, and designing the systems that have moved essential services online are, almost without exception, people who have never experienced exclusion from those systems. The divide reproduces itself through the decisions of people who don't know it exists.

What Do You Do About This?

Broadband access in rural America is a policy failure, not a market failure. The market determined that stringing cable to low-density areas is unprofitable. The government determined that universal connectivity was somebody else's problem. Forty-two million Americans lack reliable broadband access. This affects telemedicine, remote education, job applications, and small business viability. Vote for candidates who treat broadband as infrastructure.

If you live in an area with reliable internet and you're taking it for granted, go to your local library branch and watch who uses the public computers and why. Many of them are there because they don't have internet at home. They're filing for benefits. Applying for jobs. Doing homework. The divide is not abstract. It's happening in your community right now.

Don't throw away functional electronics. Your three-year-old laptop is not obsolete — it runs modern software adequately and is a tool someone without a computer could use for years. Organizations in your area accept working devices and refurbish them for distribution. Find one. Drop it off.

Public libraries are the most important digital equity infrastructure in most communities and they are being systematically defunded. They provide free internet access, computer use, digital literacy instruction, and help navigating online systems. Fund them through bond measures, attend budget hearings, and vote for politicians who prioritize them.

Digital literacy is a prerequisite for participating in the modern economy and it is not being taught uniformly. Low-income schools, rural schools, and schools serving aging populations have worse technology instruction. This produces adults who can consume content but struggle to use technology professionally, navigate bureaucratic systems online, or protect themselves from digital fraud. Advocate for funded technology education.

The digital divide intersects with age in ways deliberately ignored by technology companies. Seniors who didn't grow up with technology face significant barriers to services that have moved online — banks closing branches, government services requiring web portals, telehealth requiring apps. The frictionless future being built assumes a user base that not everyone belongs to.

Non-digital alternatives must be preserved for essential services. When your bank closes its last branch, when your benefits office eliminates phone support, when your government agency shifts entirely online, it is not neutral — it's exclusionary. Advocate for the requirement that essential services remain accessible through multiple channels, including in person and by telephone.

If you're in a position to hire, consider what your job requirements are actually testing for. 'Must be proficient in X software' can be a legitimate requirement or it can be a barrier screening out qualified people who simply didn't have access to training. The qualification is sometimes about access, not capability. The distinction matters.

The children in low-income households doing homework on their phones because they don't have a computer or reliable WiFi are not behind because of lack of effort or intelligence. They're behind because of lack of access to tools their peers have. This is a solvable resource problem being treated as an individual failure. Name it correctly.

The digital future being built assumes universal participation. The people left behind aren't opting out. They're being excluded by infrastructure decisions that prioritized profitable markets over universal access. This is a policy choice, which means it can be unmade by policy.

Chapter 19: Cyberbullying - Digital Cruelty Without Consequences

The internet gave bullies a 24/7 platform to torment their victims and an audience of millions to witness the destruction.

Traditional bullying used to end when you left school or work. Digital bullying follows you home, into your bedroom, and into your sleep. There's no escape when the harassment lives in your pocket and the tormentors can reach you anywhere you have an internet connection.

Anonymous accounts turned cowards into monsters who said things they would never dare say face-to-face. The digital mask eliminated accountability and empathy, allowing people to unleash their cruelest impulses without fear of consequences. Screen names and fake profiles gave bullies unlimited opportunities to reinvent themselves as different tormentors when their previous accounts got banned.

Group harassment campaigns coordinated through social media platforms turned individual cruelty into mob violence. Bullies organized mass reporting to get victims' accounts suspended, coordinated comment attacks to overwhelm targets with abuse, and shared personal information to enable real-world stalking and intimidation.

Swatting escalated digital harassment into life-threatening situations by making false emergency reports that sent armed police units to victims' homes. Anonymous phone calls claiming hostage situations or bomb threats turned online disagreements into potentially deadly encounters with law enforcement.

School cyberbullying followed students home and contaminated their safe spaces with digital versions of classroom cruelty. Group chats excluded targets from social plans, spread rumors faster than ever before, and created permanent digital records of humiliation that could be screenshot and shared indefinitely.

Workplace cyberbullying destroyed careers through coordinated campaigns to damage professional reputations. Bullies left fake negative reviews, spread false accusations of professional misconduct, and organized email campaigns to pressure employers to fire targeted people.

Celebrity harassment normalized the systematic abuse of public figures as entertainment for bored internet users. Coordinated attacks on actors, musicians, and public personalities created cultures where driving famous people to mental breakdowns became a form of mass entertainment.

Gaming harassment turned recreational activities into psychological warfare where players used voice chat, messaging systems, and in-game mechanics to terrorize other users. Competitive gaming communities became toxic environments where abuse was considered normal behavior and victims were blamed for being too sensitive.

Platform manipulation allowed bullies to exploit reporting systems, recommendation algorithms, and community guidelines to weaponize the platforms themselves against their targets. False reports, coordinated mass flagging, and abuse of automated moderation systems turned the platforms' own safety tools into harassment weapons.

Suicide baiting represented the most extreme form of cyberbullying where harassers explicitly encouraged victims to kill themselves, provided methods for self-harm, and celebrated when their campaigns succeeded in driving targets to suicide attempts or completion.

Identity-based harassment targeted victims for their race, gender, sexuality, religion, or disability status through coordinated campaigns of slurs, threats, and dehumanizing content. Marginalized communities faced systematic campaigns designed to drive them off platforms and out of public spaces.

Child predators used cyberbullying tactics to isolate and groom minors by systematically destroying their self-esteem, separating them from support networks, and creating dependency relationships where abuse seemed like rescue from online torment.

Corporate bullying emerged as companies used legal threats, fake accounts, and coordinated harassment to silence critics, whistleblowers, and negative reviewers. Businesses weaponized their resources to destroy people who threatened their reputations or profits.

The bystander effect amplified cyberbullying as witnesses to online harassment remained silent, shared abusive content for entertainment, or actively joined attacks to avoid becoming targets themselves. The audience participation turned individual cruelty into community-sanctioned violence.

Mental health exploitation targeted victims' psychological vulnerabilities by using their disclosed mental health struggles, trauma histories, and emotional challenges as ammunition for more effective harassment campaigns designed to trigger specific psychological responses.

Geographic harassment used victims' location data to enable real-world stalking, workplace targeting, and community-based intimidation campaigns that brought digital abuse into physical spaces where victims lived and worked.

Personal information weaponization turned everyday details about victims' lives into harassment ammunition. Bullies used family photos, work information, educational backgrounds, and social connections to create more personalized and damaging attacks that felt inescapable.

Live streaming harassment allowed bullies to torment victims in real-time while audiences watched and participated. Platforms that enabled live video became stages for public humiliation where viewers could suggest new forms of abuse and reward harassers with donations and attention.

Academic harassment targeted students and researchers through coordinated campaigns to undermine their educational achievements, discredit their work, and pressure institutions to expel or fire them based on manufactured controversies.

The platforms profited from cyberbullying by generating engagement through conflict, drama, and controversy while providing minimal resources for victim protection or bully accountability. Harassment drove traffic and advertising revenue more effectively than positive interactions.

Cyberbullying became the internet's favorite hobby, turning human cruelty into mass entertainment where destroying someone's life could make you internet-famous and harassing vulnerable people became a competitive sport with leaderboards and fan clubs.

What Do You Do About This?

If you're being harassed online, document before you do anything else. Screenshots with timestamps. Save everything before you block, because blocking can make evidence harder to retrieve later. You may need this documentation for law enforcement, platform reports, or legal action. Your instinct will be to make it stop immediately. Your strategic interest is to create a record first.

Block without guilt. Engaging with bullies — even once, even calmly — signals that engagement produces response. That signal is exactly what they're seeking. Blocking is not defeat. It's removing the reward. Do it immediately and do it completely across every platform where the harassment is occurring.

Doxxing — the publication of someone's home address, workplace, or family members' information — is harassment that can become physical danger. If you've been doxxed, report to law enforcement immediately and document what was posted and where. Contact your employer if your workplace was named. Alert family members who were identified. Many states have specific doxxing statutes. Use them.

For parents: the most important thing you can do about cyberbullying is maintain open communication before it happens. Kids don't tell parents about online harassment primarily because they're afraid of having their devices taken away. Make it explicitly clear that nothing your child tells you about online harassment will result in losing their phone. Then mean it.

Platforms have much less power over harassment than they claim. A determined harasser creates new accounts, uses VPNs, and coordinates attacks through channels the platform can't see. Platform reports are important for documentation but should not be your primary strategy. Your primary strategies are removing yourself from the harasser's reach and, when threats are made, involving law enforcement.

Anonymous harassment is not as anonymous as it appears. IP addresses, device fingerprints, metadata in screenshots, coordination patterns across accounts — skilled investigators can frequently identify anonymous harassers. Law enforcement agencies increasingly have cybercrime units equipped to do this. If threats are made, report them.

If the harassment is happening to someone you know, don't just express sympathy. Ask specifically what they need. Often the answer is a witness — someone to sit with them while they document, someone to help think through options, someone who isn't minimizing it. Showing up concretely is more useful than expressing horror from a distance.

The psychological impact of coordinated online harassment is documented and serious. It produces PTSD symptoms, depression, anxiety, and in extreme cases suicidal ideation. It is not 'just the internet.' The threats are about your real life. The humiliation is experienced in your real brain. Take it seriously and get professional support rather than trying to white-knuckle through it.

Teen cyberbullying requires a different response than adult cyberbullying. Schools have legal obligations and can implement real consequences that social platforms often won't. Know your school district's cyberbullying policy. If they don't have one, attend the next school board meeting and ask why.

Building a life that's not primarily lived online is the strongest long-term protection against cyberbullying. Harassers' power comes from their ability to reach you where you spend time. The smaller the proportion of your life that's online, the smaller their reach. Real-world community, real-world relationships, and real-world accomplishments are things they cannot touch.

Chapter 20: Cyberterrorism - Digital Weapons of Mass Disruption

The internet gave terrorists new ways to destroy critical infrastructure, cripple entire economies, and kill people without ever leaving their computers.

Critical infrastructure hacking turned power grids, water treatment plants, and transportation systems into terrorist targets that could be attacked remotely from anywhere in the world. A single successful cyberattack on electrical systems could kill more people than a traditional bombing by shutting down hospitals, traffic systems, and emergency services.

Hospital system attacks weaponized healthcare by encrypting patient records, disabling life support systems, and shutting down emergency services during medical crises. Ransomware attacks on medical facilities forced doctors to choose between paying terrorist demands or watching patients die from lack of access to their own medical equipment.

Financial system terrorism paralyzed banking networks, stock exchanges, and payment processing systems to create economic chaos and undermine public confidence in monetary institutions. Cyberterrorists discovered they could cause more economic damage with computer code than with physical explosives.

Transportation grid attacks targeted air traffic control systems, railway networks, and shipping logistics to create travel chaos and supply chain disruptions. Terrorists learned that shutting down transportation hubs could strand millions of people and paralyze commerce more effectively than traditional attacks.

Water supply contamination through industrial control system hacking threatened to poison entire cities by manipulating chemical treatment processes, opening contamination valves, and disabling safety monitoring systems. Digital attacks on water infrastructure could kill thousands without terrorists ever touching physical facilities.

Nuclear facility targeting represented the ultimate cyberterrorism threat as attackers attempted to cause meltdowns, radiation releases, and catastrophic accidents by compromising reactor control systems and safety mechanisms designed to prevent nuclear disasters.

Emergency services disruption attacked 911 systems, police communication networks, and fire department dispatch systems to prevent first responders from coordinating during crises. Terrorists maximized damage from other attacks by ensuring that emergency response would be delayed or impossible.

Media hijacking allowed terrorists to take control of television broadcasts, radio stations, and digital billboards to spread propaganda, false information, and panic-inducing messages to millions of people simultaneously during coordinated attack campaigns.

School system attacks targeted educational institutions through ransomware, data theft, and system shutdowns designed to disrupt education and traumatize children. Terrorists discovered that attacking schools generated maximum public fear and political pressure with minimal technical effort.

Supply chain warfare poisoned global commerce by infiltrating manufacturing systems, shipping networks, and inventory management platforms to disrupt the flow of goods, contaminate products, and create shortages of essential supplies.

Internet infrastructure attacks targeted the backbone systems that keep the internet functioning, including domain name servers, routing systems, and fiber optic networks. Terrorists attempted to shut down entire regions' internet access to isolate populations and prevent communication.

Satellite system hijacking threatened GPS navigation, communication satellites, and weather monitoring systems that modern civilization depends on for everything from agriculture to aviation. Space-based terrorism could blind entire continents to approaching storms and disable global positioning systems.

Psychological warfare through cyberterrorism amplified the fear and disruption caused by attacks by targeting civilian populations with threatening messages, fake emergency alerts, and misinformation designed to create panic and undermine social cohesion.

Recruitment and radicalization networks used social media platforms, encrypted messaging apps, and gaming communities to identify vulnerable people and gradually convert them to terrorist ideologies through sophisticated psychological manipulation campaigns.

Crowdsourced terrorism coordinated distributed attacks by recruiting thousands of sympathizers to participate in simultaneous cyberattacks that overwhelmed defensive systems through sheer volume rather than sophisticated techniques.

Dark web terrorism marketplaces sold hacking tools, attack methods, and target information to enable less technically skilled terrorists to launch sophisticated attacks using purchased capabilities from criminal organizations.

Artificial intelligence weapons development created autonomous attack systems that could identify targets, adapt to defensive measures, and execute complex attacks without human oversight, representing a new generation of digital weapons with unprecedented destructive potential.

IoT device weaponization turned everyday connected devices into attack platforms by compromising smart home systems, medical devices, and industrial sensors to create massive botnets capable of overwhelming any target with coordinated attacks.

State-sponsored cyberterrorism blurred the lines between terrorism and warfare as nation-states used terrorist tactics, proxy groups, and plausible deniability to attack enemy infrastructure while avoiding traditional military responses to their aggression.

The internet created the perfect terrorism platform by providing global reach, minimal cost, plausible deniability, and maximum disruption potential for groups that previously needed extensive resources and physical presence to threaten civilized society.

What Do You Do About This?

Ransomware attacks on hospitals have caused patient deaths. In 2020, a ransomware attack on Düsseldorf University Hospital forced the diversion of emergency patients and contributed to at least one death, though establishing direct causation in court proved complicated. The causal chain is real regardless: systems go down, care gets disrupted, outcomes get worse. When people argue that cyberattacks don't cause physical harm, they haven't been paying attention.

Your local hospital, water utility, and power company are probably less secure than you think. Critical infrastructure cybersecurity in the United States is voluntary in many sectors and underfunded in most. The 2021 Colonial Pipeline attack shut down fuel distribution across the Southeast for six days because a major pipeline company had inadequate basic security. These are resource and priority failures, not inevitable technical limitations.

Personal preparedness for infrastructure disruption is appropriate, not paranoid. Keep enough water stored for 72 hours. Keep food that doesn't require refrigeration or cooking. Keep cash on hand because ATMs and card readers go down during power outages. Keep physical copies of essential documents. These preparations apply to any infrastructure disruption, cyber-caused or otherwise.

Paying ransomware demands funds the next attack. When companies and hospitals pay ransoms to get their systems back, they're financing the operations that will attack the next hospital. The ethical case against paying is strong. The practical case for it when systems are down and people are at risk is equally strong. This is a genuine dilemma without a clean answer.

Nation-state cyberterrorism is not a hypothetical future threat. Russian cyberattacks shut down Ukraine's power grid in 2015 and 2016. Iranian attacks targeted US financial institutions and Saudi oil infrastructure. North Korean attacks on financial systems funded their weapons programs. The attacks that made the news are not the only ones happening. They are the ones that happened to get disclosed.

The most important thing you can do about infrastructure cybersecurity is vote for politicians who treat it as serious infrastructure investment. The same way you vote for politicians who maintain roads and bridges, vote for politicians who mandate security standards for critical infrastructure, fund cybersecurity education, and hold companies to enforceable standards.

Disinformation campaigns are part of cyberterrorism's toolkit. When an attack happens — or even when one is claimed — coordinated disinformation spreads to amplify the panic and distrust that are the attack's actual goals. Pause before sharing any breaking news about infrastructure attacks. Verify through official channels. Don't amplify unverified reports.

Small and medium businesses are soft targets that provide entry points to larger targets through their supply chains. If you own or manage a business of any size, basic cybersecurity hygiene — separate business and personal accounts, current backups, employee security training, multi-factor authentication — is not optional anymore. You're not just protecting yourself.

Volunteer for your local emergency management organization. These organizations plan for infrastructure disruption and they're chronically underfunded and understaffed. The community resilience that protects people when infrastructure fails is built before disasters, not during them.

The fear cyberterrorism is designed to produce is sometimes more damaging than the attack itself. Uncertainty about whether the power will stay on, whether the water is safe, whether the financial system is stable — this psychological disruption is what most attacks aim for. Being informed, prepared, and connected to local community is more protective than monitoring every cyberthreat report obsessively.

Chapter 21: Cyberwarfare - The Invisible Battlefield

On December 23, 2015, engineers at three Ukrainian electricity distribution companies watched their cursors move across their screens by themselves. Someone else had control. Within thirty minutes, attackers — later attributed to Sandworm, a unit of Russian military intelligence — had switched off substations serving roughly 230,000 people. It was the middle of winter. At the same moment the power went out, the attackers flooded the utilities' customer service lines with automated calls, making it impossible for staff to process real emergency reports. They had wiped the firmware on the substation control devices so operators couldn't restore power remotely. Recovery required engineers to drive out in the dark and switch everything back by hand. The lights came back on after one to six hours. The attackers had been inside the networks for months before they acted, mapping the systems, learning the layout, waiting.

That is what cyberwarfare actually looks like. Not a movie hacker typing furiously in a dark room. A military unit, operating from desks in another country, conducting a months-long intelligence operation against civilian infrastructure, then executing a coordinated attack timed for maximum damage, followed by countermeasures designed to slow recovery. No soldiers crossed a border. No missiles were fired. No war was declared. The people who lost heat that night had no idea any of it was happening until the lights went out. Ukraine's government knew who did it. Russia denied it. Nothing happened.

Military systems hacking turned defense infrastructure into vulnerabilities as enemy nations infiltrated missile defense systems, drone networks, and communication satellites to disable military capabilities or turn weapons against their own operators.

Economic warfare through cyberattacks allowed countries to cripple enemy economies by targeting banking systems, stock exchanges, and currency markets to cause financial collapse without traditional military invasion or siege tactics.

Election interference reached new levels of sophistication as nation-states used social media manipulation, voter database hacking, and disinformation campaigns to destabilize democratic processes and install favorable political leaders in enemy countries.

The Russian Internet Research Agency's 2016 operation against the American election is the clearest documented case of what this looks like at scale. Three thousand ads. Hundreds of fake accounts. Tens of millions of impressions. Content designed not to promote a candidate but to amplify division — Black Lives Matter content served to Black Americans, anti-immigrant content served to conservative voters, veteran content, gun content, content about police, content calibrated by psychological profile and ZIP code to find exactly the right nerve to press. The goal wasn't to change minds. It was to deepen the fractures that already existed until Americans were too busy fighting each other to notice who was running the operation. The power grid attack cuts the lights for a night. The Facebook operation cuts something harder to restore. Both are warfare. One leaves you cold until morning. The other leaves you unable to trust what you read for years.

Intelligence gathering operations penetrated government networks, military communications, and diplomatic correspondence to steal state secrets, military plans, and negotiation strategies that provided enormous advantages in international relations.

Industrial espionage campaigns targeted trade secrets, manufacturing processes, and technological innovations to steal decades of research and development work, allowing aggressor nations to advance their capabilities while damaging competitor economies.

Propaganda warfare used social media algorithms, fake news networks, and influencer operations to manipulate public opinion in enemy countries, turning citizens against their own governments and sowing discord within allied populations.

Sabotage operations remotely destroyed manufacturing facilities, research laboratories, and development projects by infiltrating industrial control systems and causing equipment failures, explosions, and contamination incidents.

Proxy warfare allowed nations to attack enemies through criminal organizations, terrorist groups, and supposedly independent hacker collectives while maintaining plausible deniability about their involvement in acts of digital aggression.

Supply chain infiltration compromised hardware and software components during manufacturing to create backdoors, vulnerabilities, and kill switches that could be activated during conflicts to disable enemy systems remotely.

Space warfare extended into cyberspace as nations developed capabilities to hack satellites, disable GPS systems, and disrupt space-based communications that modern militaries depend on for navigation, timing, and coordination.

Civil infrastructure targeting turned power grids, transportation networks, and communication systems into military objectives that could be destroyed digitally to cause civilian casualties and undermine enemy morale and capabilities.

Diplomatic network penetration allowed nations to monitor international negotiations, steal bargaining strategies, and manipulate diplomatic communications to gain advantages in treaties, trade deals, and international agreements.

Nuclear command infiltration represented the ultimate cyberwarfare objective as nations attempted to hack into enemy nuclear weapons systems to prevent retaliation during conflicts or potentially cause accidental launches that would trigger devastating responses.

Allied network compromise turned friendly nations into attack platforms by infiltrating their systems and using their infrastructure to launch attacks that appeared to come from allies rather than actual adversaries.

Medical system warfare targeted enemy healthcare infrastructure to overwhelm hospitals during conflicts, steal biological research, and potentially release biological agents through compromised laboratory systems.

Educational institution targeting aimed to steal research, recruit spies, and disrupt education systems that train future leaders, scientists, and military personnel in enemy countries.

Financial market manipulation allowed nations to cause stock market crashes, currency devaluations, and banking failures in enemy countries while simultaneously profiting from the economic chaos through carefully timed investments.

Resource allocation warfare disrupted enemy supply chains, shipping networks, and resource distribution systems to create shortages of essential materials and undermine industrial production capabilities.

Social media weaponization turned platforms into battlefields where nations deployed bot armies, fake accounts, and algorithmic manipulation to control information flows and shape public discourse in enemy territories.

The internet erased geographical boundaries for warfare, allowing small nations to attack superpowers, enabling simultaneous conflicts on every continent, and making every civilian device a potential weapon in an invisible war that never ends.

What Do You Do About This?

Election infrastructure is under constant attack and has been since at least 2016. The Senate Intelligence Committee's bipartisan report documented Russian interference across all fifty states during the 2016 election. State-level voting infrastructure, campaign systems, and voter registration databases are all targets. Actual voting machines in most jurisdictions are not connected to the internet. Everything around them is vulnerable.

The SolarWinds attack — discovered in 2020 — compromised eighteen thousand organizations including the Treasury Department, the Pentagon, and multiple federal agencies. Attackers had access for months before detection. This is documented. The U.S. government itself is regularly penetrated by sophisticated nation-state actors. Your data held by government agencies is not secure by default.

Two-factor authentication on every account you care about is not optional anymore. Nation-state and criminal actors use credential-stuffing attacks — taking passwords exposed in one breach and testing them across thousands of sites. If your email password is the same as any other password you've used in the last ten years, change it. Use a password manager. Use different passwords everywhere.

The distinction between cyberwarfare and cybercrime is legally real but psychologically irrelevant to victims. Whether a ransomware attack on your hospital came from a nation-state or a criminal gang, the results are the same. The tools, techniques, and frequent collaboration between state actors and criminal organizations mean the categories blur in practice. Defend against both.

Disinformation is a cyberwarfare weapon deployed against your cognition specifically. The goal of foreign influence operations is not to make you believe specific false things — it's to make you unable to believe anything reliably. The response is developing the habit of sitting with uncertainty rather than resolving it through the first emotionally satisfying narrative.

Your phone is a collection device. Every major smartphone operating system has been the subject of nation-state exploitation. Pegasus spyware infected phones through zero-click exploits requiring no action from the target. If you're a journalist, activist, lawyer, or work in sensitive industries, your threat model is different from an average user's. Know what you are and protect accordingly.

VPNs are useful but not magic. A VPN protects your traffic from your internet service provider and hides your IP address from the sites you visit. It does not protect you from malware on your device, from the VPN company itself, or from sophisticated nation-state actors. Use a reputable VPN for privacy from your ISP. Don't treat it as a comprehensive security guarantee.

The economic cyberwarfare being waged between nations affects your retirement account, your job, and the prices you pay even though you'll never see the connection. Attacks on financial systems, supply chains, and industrial operations have downstream effects throughout the economy. This is ongoing conflict with material costs.

Support diplomatic efforts to establish cyberwarfare norms while maintaining realistic expectations about compliance. Imperfect international agreements are better than no agreements, and they create political costs for violations even when enforcement is weak.

You are not helpless in the face of nation-state threats. The basic security measures — updated software, strong unique passwords, two-factor authentication, skepticism toward unexpected emails — protect against the majority of attacks including those by sophisticated actors who prefer soft targets. Be a harder target.

Chapter 22: Cybercrime - The Digital Wild West

A woman in her late sixties met a man online. He was a widowed engineer working overseas — or so he said. They talked every day for eight months. He sent photos. He remembered her birthday. He asked about her grandchildren by name. When he finally asked for money — a medical emergency, he said, just temporary, he would pay her back — she sent it. Then he needed more. Then more after that. By the time her daughter sat her down and showed her the evidence — the stock photos he'd used as his face, the documented scam operation running out of West Africa — she had sent over two hundred thousand dollars. Her retirement savings. The equity from a refinanced house.

Her daughter thought showing her the proof would end it. It didn't. The woman sent more money. The man had a ready answer for the accusation: her family was jealous. Her family wanted to keep her isolated. He was the only one who truly cared about her. She believed him over the people who had known her for decades, because the alternative was accepting that the most intimate relationship she'd had in years was a fabrication run by a criminal who had never thought of her as a human being.

That story is not unusual. Versions of it appear in FBI fraud reports every year, in numbers that keep climbing, from victims who are not stupid or gullible by any normal measure. They are targeted by professionals whose full-time job is learning exactly how to build trust, manufacture emotional dependency, and then exploit it. The internet made this scalable. One operation, working from a building in another country, can run dozens of these relationships simultaneously, shift to a new set of victims when the first runs dry, and face essentially no meaningful risk of prosecution.

That is the structural fact that explains cybercrime: the internet separated criminals from victims geographically while law enforcement remained local. A thief who steals a wallet in

Chicago faces Chicago police, Illinois courts, and federal jurisdiction if the theft crosses state lines. A criminal who drains a Chicago woman's retirement account from Lagos faces none of those things. The FBI has an Internet Crime Complaint Center. It receives nearly a million complaints a year and prosecutes a fraction of a percent of them. Not because investigators aren't working hard. Because the architecture of the internet was built for open exchange, not law enforcement, and the criminals figured that out before the legislators did.

Romance scams are the most damaging category by dollar amount because they destroy something beyond money. The FBI reported over a billion dollars in losses from romance fraud in a single year — and that number reflects only what gets reported, which researchers estimate at under 15% of actual losses. The victims don't report because they're ashamed, because part of them still doesn't fully believe it, and because reporting means saying out loud that the most meaningful relationship they had wasn't real. The criminals count on the silence.

Pig butchering — the name comes from the practice of fattening a pig before slaughter — is the long-con evolution of the romance scam. The criminal spends weeks or months building a genuine relationship before introducing a cryptocurrency investment opportunity. The victim sees real returns at first, because the platform is fake and the criminal controls what the dashboard shows. When the victim tries to withdraw, there are fees to pay, taxes to clear, accounts to verify. They keep paying until there's nothing left. The emotional investment and the financial investment reinforce each other. Losing the money means losing the relationship. So they lose both.

Sextortion runs the same emotional lever from the other direction. The criminal solicits intimate images, or manufactures them using deepfake technology, then threatens to send them to the victim's employer, family, and friends unless payment is made. The threat works because the shame is real whether the images are or not. Teenagers have died by suicide after receiving these threats. The criminals, almost universally operating from overseas, continue operating.

Business email compromise exploits something different: not loneliness but the reasonable assumption that official-looking communications from known senders are legitimate. An employee receives an email that appears to come from the CEO asking for an urgent wire transfer. The formatting is right, the email address looks right, the request is plausible. The FBI estimated losses from BEC at over two and a half billion dollars in a single year. The defense is a phone call — verify any unusual wire request through a known number, not a number in the email. Most companies don't have that policy. Most that do don't enforce it consistently. That gap is the criminal's entry point.

Tech support scams run the same institutional trust playbook at the individual level. A popup announces that your computer is infected and provides a number to call. A helpful technician walks you through granting remote access to your machine to clean the infection. There is no infection. The technician is installing malware, harvesting credentials, or simply charging hundreds of dollars for the service. The scam works because Microsoft and Apple really do provide support, the popups look official, and older users in particular have been trained to take computer warnings seriously.

Fake government agency fraud calls the same trust into service. The IRS will arrest you for unpaid taxes. Social Security has suspended your number. Customs has seized a package with your name on it. Pay now to resolve it. The threats are lies, but they work because government agencies do contact people for exactly these reasons, and the fear of legal trouble overrides skepticism. The criminal doesn't need the caller to be certain it's real. They need the caller to be uncertain it's fake.

Employment scams target people who are already losing. You respond to a job listing that looks real — a company name, a salary, a job description. The hiring process is conducted entirely by email or chat. You get the offer. Then you need to pay for training materials, background check fees, or equipment. The company doesn't exist. The listing was scraped from a real job board and reposted. Desperate people looking for work pay criminals for the experience of being hired and then ghosted.

Advance fee fraud — the Nigerian prince scheme, updated — still extracts money from people who know about it, because the modern versions are personalized in ways the original wasn't. You've been selected for a grant. Your unclaimed inheritance requires processing fees. An investment opportunity requires a small bridge payment to unlock the larger return. The emotional architecture is identical to the romance scam: the criminal creates belief in a windfall, then charges fees to release it, then invents reasons why additional fees are required. The fees never stop because the windfall never arrives.

Medical fraud finds people who are sick, frightened, and running out of options. Fake clinics, counterfeit medications, supplements that promise cures for conditions medicine can't fully treat — cancer, chronic pain, autoimmune disorders. The victims aren't irrational. They're desperate, and desperation is a known, exploitable psychological state. The criminals who sell fake treatments to terminal patients are running the same operation as every other cybercriminal. They've just selected for the most vulnerable possible target population.

Cryptocurrency didn't create cybercrime. It industrialized it. Before cryptocurrency, criminals needed to move money through banks, which created records and triggered reporting requirements. Crypto is pseudonymous, borderless, and irreversible — which means a successful theft cannot be unwound even when the criminal is identified. Ransomware attacks, romance scams, drug markets, money laundering, and fraud all run on crypto infrastructure because it solved the criminal's hardest problem: getting the money out.

Gift cards became criminal currency for a simpler reason: they're untraceable and the value is immediately accessible anywhere. Every gift card scam — pay your utility bill in Target gift cards, resolve your legal problem with iTunes codes, claim your prize with Google Play redemption numbers — works because gift cards can't be recalled, disputed, or frozen. The instruction to buy gift cards is now widely recognized as a scam signal. Criminals keep using them because enough people still comply.

Identity theft sits underneath all of this as infrastructure. Your stolen credentials don't just allow criminals to open fraudulent accounts in your name. They allow other criminals to impersonate you in ways you won't discover for months: tax returns filed before yours, medical procedures billed to your insurance, employment records that follow you into background checks. The market for stolen identity data is organized, tiered by quality, and priced accordingly. Your Social Security number combined with your date of birth and mother's maiden name sells for a few dollars. Your complete financial profile sells for more.

The woman who lost her retirement savings never got the money back. The man she thought she loved was never found. Law enforcement in her state did what they could, which wasn't much, because the operation was in another country, the accounts had been emptied through cryptocurrency mixers, and there were hundreds of other active cases with the same profile. She knows now it was a scam. She knows it intellectually. The knowledge doesn't fully displace eight months of daily conversation, remembered birthdays, and the feeling of being seen by someone.

That's what cybercrime actually is, underneath the technical descriptions and the crime-type categories. It's the systematic exploitation of the things that make people human — loneliness, trust, hope, fear, the desire to be loved, the fear of authority, the desperation of illness, the vulnerability of age. The internet didn't invent those vulnerabilities. It gave people with no conscience and no accountability a way to reach every person who has them, from anywhere in the world, at scale, with near-zero risk. The geography that used to protect people from most criminals no longer applies. The law enforcement that used to constrain most criminals hasn't caught up. The gap between those two facts is where the industry lives.

What Do You Do About This?

The woman described at the start of this chapter kept sending money after her family showed her proof of the scam. That isn't stupidity. That's what eight months of daily emotional investment does to a person's judgment, and the criminals who run these operations understand it completely. The rule is simple and must be treated as absolute: never send money to someone you have not met in person, regardless of how long you've been talking, how real the relationship feels, or what explanation they give for why meeting isn't possible. The feeling is real. The person almost certainly isn't.

The grandparent scam — a call claiming your grandchild is in jail and needs bail money wired immediately — depletes life savings every day. Call your grandchild directly before sending a dollar. Call another family member. Do not send gift cards. Do not wire money. Do not call back the number that called you. This advice sounds obvious and thousands of people who know it are victimized because the emotional manipulation is sophisticated and the caller is professional.

Business email compromise — where criminals impersonate executives or vendors to redirect wire transfers — cost businesses over \$2.7 billion in one year. The defense is phone verification. Any request to change payment information or wire money to a new account must be verified by calling the requestor at a known number, not a number provided in the email. This one procedure, applied consistently, stops almost all BEC attacks.

Cryptocurrency enables cybercrime at scale because it's irreversible, pseudonymous, and crosses jurisdictions smoothly. Every cryptocurrency investment opportunity from a stranger online is a scam. Pig butchering scams — where criminals build relationships before steering victims into fake investment platforms — extracted billions from American victims in recent years alone. When cryptocurrency and guaranteed returns appear together, close the conversation.

Identity theft recovery takes years and affects credit, employment, housing, and tax filings. Freeze your credit at all three bureaus now, not after a breach. A credit freeze is free, prevents new accounts from being opened in your name, and can be temporarily lifted when you need it. Virtually every personal finance expert recommends this. Very few people do it until after they're victimized.

Free public WiFi is a target-rich environment for criminals running man-in-the-middle attacks. If you're accessing any financial account, health record, or sensitive system, use your phone's cellular connection or a VPN, not the hotel WiFi or coffee shop network. The inconvenience is minor. The exposure on an unsecured network is significant.

Cybercrime is heavily underreported because victims are embarrassed. The Social Security fraud victim doesn't call the police because they feel stupid. The romance scam victim doesn't report because they feel humiliated. Report to IC3.gov regardless. The underreporting means criminals operate with impunity because law enforcement doesn't have the data to allocate resources appropriately.

Your personal information is for sale on the dark web right now, probably including your email, password hashes, and possibly your Social Security number. This is the documented result of thousands of corporate data breaches. Use haveibeenpwned.com to see which breaches included your email address. Change any password that appeared in a breach.

Phishing has replaced most other attack vectors because it works. Security researchers consistently find that between 15% and 30% of employees will click a convincing phishing link. The defense is not better spam filters. The defense is slow, deliberate action around any communication requesting credentials or financial action. Pause. Verify through an independent channel. Then act.

Cybercrime is not a technology problem. It's a human psychology problem exploited through technology. The attacks that succeed don't beat security systems — they beat people. They exploit urgency, fear, greed, loneliness, and trust. Learn your own vulnerabilities. Know when you're being pushed toward urgency, because urgency is the attacker's most reliable weapon.

Chapter 23: Hacktivism - Digital Vigilantes

Anonymous hackers decided they were the internet's police force, judge, and jury, dispensing digital justice according to their own moral codes and political agendas.

Distributed denial of service attacks became the protest method of choice for digital activists who could shut down websites by overwhelming them with traffic from thousands of compromised computers. Online sit-ins replaced physical demonstrations as hacktivists discovered they could paralyze organizations without leaving their bedrooms.

Website defacements turned corporate and government homepages into political billboards where hacktivists posted manifestos, protest messages, and embarrassing information about their targets. Digital graffiti became a form of political expression.

Social media hijacking allowed hacktivists to take control of official accounts belonging to politicians, corporations, and organizations to spread their own messages through established channels with large follower bases.

Database dumping published personal information about police officers, government officials, and corporate executives as retaliation for policies and actions the hacktivists opposed. Private information became weapons in political warfare.

Operation payback campaigns targeted organizations that hacktivists perceived as enemies of internet freedom, free speech, or social justice. Credit card companies, law firms, and government agencies became targets of coordinated cyberattacks.

Anonymous operations coordinated global hacktivist campaigns against targets ranging from the Church of Scientology to authoritarian governments. The decentralized movement launched cyberattacks while hiding behind masks and pseudonyms that made prosecution nearly impossible.

WikiLeaks revolutionized hacktivist journalism by providing platforms for whistleblowers to publish classified documents, diplomatic cables, and corporate secrets that exposed government and corporate wrongdoing to global audiences.

Leak site proliferation created dozens of platforms where hacktivists could publish stolen documents, internal communications, and confidential information while protecting the anonymity of both sources and publishers.

Virtual blockades used coordinated cyberattacks to prevent organizations from conducting normal business operations, forcing them to address hacktivist demands or face continued disruption of their digital infrastructure.

The hacktivist movement created digital vigilantes who appointed themselves as arbiters of justice in cyberspace, deciding which organizations deserved to be punished and which secrets deserved to be exposed according to their personal political beliefs.

What Do You Do About This?

Anonymous was never a coherent organization with accountable leadership. It was a label adopted by whoever wanted to use it for whatever purpose they chose that week. Operations done under the Anonymous banner included exposing child pornography networks and attacking game companies over copyright disputes. Evaluating 'Anonymous' as a thing requires evaluating specific operations, not the brand.

WikiLeaks served a genuine public interest function in 2010 with the Iraq War Logs and the Collateral Murder video. It served a different function in 2016 when it published Democratic National Committee emails timed to maximum electoral damage with what intelligence agencies concluded was Russian government assistance. These are not the same organization doing the same thing. Time, relationships, and context changed what WikiLeaks was. Evaluate accordingly.

DDoS attacks cause real collateral damage that attackers typically don't account for. When hacktivists attacked PayPal over its WikiLeaks payment processing decision, they disrupted payments for millions of unrelated businesses and people. The political target was chosen. The collateral damage was random. This pattern repeats consistently in hacktivist operations.

Information released through hacks should be verified before you treat it as fact. Stolen information can be selectively released, altered, or published out of context. Every piece of information released through hacktivist operations should be treated with the same skepticism you'd apply to opposition research — which is essentially what it often is.

The legal consequences of hacktivist participation are real and frequently disproportionate. The Computer Fraud and Abuse Act imposes criminal penalties that turn minor technical violations into felonies. People who participated peripherally in Anonymous operations have served real prison sentences. Moral righteousness is not a legal defense.

Whistleblowing and hacking are not the same thing legally or ethically. Daniel Ellsberg releasing the Pentagon Papers — documents he had authorized access to — is a different moral category from breaking into a system to take information. The moral weight of disclosure depends heavily on the method of acquisition.

The people most harmed by large data dumps are usually not the intended targets. WikiLeaks' release of diplomatic cables included the names of dissidents, sources, and activists in authoritarian countries. People were endangered. The decision to release everything rather than redact had human consequences.

The moral case for vigilante justice online is the same as for vigilante justice offline — sometimes the system fails and sometimes the action produces good outcomes. It doesn't generalize cleanly, it doesn't provide accountability, and it doesn't protect against abuse by people who adopt the same tactics for different ends.

The hacktivist operations that feel most righteous in the moment often look different in retrospect. The moral clarity of fighting for the right side against the wrong side assumes you've correctly identified which side is which. Intelligence services of multiple countries have run operations under hacktivist cover.

Legitimate channels for exposing wrongdoing — journalists, regulatory agencies, inspectors general, congressional oversight — are slow, bureaucratic, and frequently inadequate. They are also the structures that provide some accountability for who gets to decide what wrongdoing deserves exposure. They're worth improving before abandoning for systems with no accountability at all.

Chapter 24: Cyber Espionage - Digital Spies

A journalist who had been critical of the Saudi government was communicating with sources, planning his next piece, keeping his work private through encrypted messaging. His phone had been compromised months earlier. The spyware installed on it — sold by an Israeli surveillance company to foreign governments, used here by Saudi intelligence — didn't require him to click a link or open a file. It arrived through a zero-click exploit, a vulnerability in the phone's software that required no action from the target. From that point forward, his calls, his messages, his location, his contacts, his camera, his microphone — all of it was accessible to the people who wanted to know what he knew and who he knew it with. When he walked into the Saudi consulate in Istanbul in October 2018, he didn't walk out. Whether the intelligence gathered from his phone directly enabled what happened inside that building has never been fully established. What is established is that the people who ordered his killing had been reading his private communications for months before they acted.

That is the argument for why cyber espionage is different from the espionage that came before it. Traditional intelligence required a human asset with physical access — someone inside the target's circle, able to see documents, overhear conversations, report back. That took years to develop and carried enormous risk. Pegasus required a phone number and a government with a license. The target doesn't need to do anything. They don't need to click a link. The device is owned, and everything on it flows back to whoever paid for the capability. The journalist didn't know. His sources didn't know. The people who died because of what that surveillance revealed didn't know. Espionage at this scale, at this cost, with this level of deniability, didn't exist before the internet. It exists now because a market emerged to sell it, governments lined up to buy it, and no international framework has managed to regulate it.

The internet turned every computer, smartphone, and connected device into a potential spy that could be recruited by intelligence agencies, foreign governments, and criminal organizations.

Corporate espionage moved into cyberspace where competitors could steal trade secrets, research information, and strategic plans through network infiltration rather than planting human spies in target companies. Decades of research could be stolen in minutes.

Government intelligence gathering expanded exponentially as intelligence agencies gained access to email communications and digital records that revealed more about citizens' lives than traditional surveillance ever could.

Foreign intelligence operations penetrated domestic networks to steal government secrets, military plans, and technological innovations while mapping critical infrastructure for potential future attacks during conflicts or negotiations.

Academic espionage targeted universities and research institutions to steal scientific discoveries, technological breakthroughs, and intellectual property that foreign nations could use to advance their own capabilities.

Supply chain infiltration allowed spies to compromise hardware and software components during manufacturing, creating backdoors and surveillance capabilities that remained hidden until activated by intelligence agencies.

Insider threat programs turned employees into unwitting intelligence assets through blackmail, financial incentives, or ideological persuasion that convinced them to steal information from their own organizations.

Economic espionage targeted financial institutions, trading firms, and economic policy makers to gain advance knowledge of market moves, policy decisions, and competitive strategies that provided enormous financial advantages.

Diplomatic espionage intercepted communications between foreign governments, international organizations, and diplomatic missions to gain negotiating advantages and advance knowledge of other nations' positions and strategies.

Military technology theft focused on defense contractors, weapons manufacturers, and military research facilities to steal advanced technology designs, tactical information, and strategic capabilities that took years and billions of dollars to develop.

Healthcare intelligence collected medical records, genetic information, and pharmaceutical research to identify biological vulnerabilities, steal drug development research, and build detailed health profiles of targeted populations.

Energy sector espionage targeted oil companies, utility providers, and renewable energy developers to steal geological information, infrastructure plans, and technological innovations related to energy production and distribution.

Communications interception programs monitored phone calls, text messages, and internet communications through partnerships with telecommunications providers and direct network infiltration that captured massive amounts of private communications.

Facial recognition surveillance combined stolen photo databases with artificial intelligence to track people across multiple platforms and physical locations, creating comprehensive movement and association profiles.

Financial intelligence operations monitored banking transactions, investment activities, and economic communications to identify money laundering, track terrorist financing, and gather intelligence about foreign economic activities.

Cryptocurrency surveillance tracked digital currency transactions to identify criminal activity, monitor sanctions evasion, and gather intelligence about financial activities that users believed were anonymous and untraceable.

Cloud storage infiltration gave intelligence agencies access to personal documents, photos, and communications that people stored on remote servers owned by technology companies that cooperated with government surveillance requests.

IoT device exploitation turned smart home devices, connected cars, and wearable technology into surveillance tools that could monitor conversations, track movements, and collect intimate details about daily life.

Metadata collection gathered information about communications patterns, location information, and digital activities without accessing actual content, creating detailed profiles of relationships, movements, and behaviors.

Zero-day exploit development created secret vulnerabilities in widely used software that intelligence agencies could use to gain unauthorized access to target systems while keeping the vulnerabilities secret from software vendors.

Biometric harvesting collected fingerprints, facial recognition information, and other biological identifiers from various sources to create comprehensive identification databases that could track people across multiple systems and locations.

Satellite surveillance combined with cyber intelligence to monitor global communications, track vehicle movements, and observe activities that targets believed were private or unmonitored.

AI-powered analysis processed vast amounts of collected intelligence to identify patterns, predict behaviors, and automatically flag people or activities of interest to human analysts and decision-makers.

The digital age created the most comprehensive surveillance apparatus in human history, where every click, search, and digital transaction could be monitored, analyzed, and stored by intelligence agencies that operated in shadows.

What Do You Do About This?

The NSA is reading your metadata. Not your content in most cases, but who you called, when, how long, from where, and to whom. This is documented by the Snowden disclosures and confirmed by subsequent court decisions. The metadata reveals your doctor, your lawyer, your religious affiliation, your political activity, and your intimate relationships. The claim that 'metadata isn't personal' is false.

Corporate espionage through cyberspace costs American businesses an estimated $600 billion per year. The primary attackers are China, Russia, Iran, and North Korea — nation-state actors pursuing industrial intelligence for national economic advantage. If you work in biotech, defense, energy, finance, or advanced manufacturing, your employer is a target.

Pegasus spyware — sold by NSO Group to governments worldwide — infected thousands of phones through vulnerabilities requiring zero interaction from the target. Journalists, lawyers, activists, and heads of state were targeted. The spyware gave complete access to messages, camera, microphone, and location. This happened. It's documented.

Keep your phone's operating system updated. Zero-day vulnerabilities — security flaws not yet publicly disclosed — are worth millions on both legitimate bug bounty markets and underground markets. Vendors patch known vulnerabilities in operating system updates. When you delay updates, you're leaving known vulnerabilities open.

If you work in a sensitive field and travel internationally, treat your devices as potentially compromised when you return. Several countries — China specifically, but not exclusively — have documented programs of device compromise at border crossings and in hotel rooms. Bring a clean travel laptop. Leave sensitive data at home.

Supply chain attacks are among the most sophisticated and hardest to defend against. The SolarWinds attackers didn't break into their targets directly — they compromised a software update mechanism and rode it into thousands of organizations. Your software supply chain is an attack surface. This is an argument for using major software from companies with significant security investment.

End-to-end encrypted messaging — Signal, specifically — is the strongest protection available for message content against most adversaries. When encryption is done correctly, even the company operating the service cannot read your messages. Signal's entire codebase is open source and independently audited. Use it for sensitive communications.

Your smart home devices — speakers, cameras, thermostats, doorbells — are network-connected computers with minimal security investment and potentially permanent presence in your most private spaces. Several have been compromised in ways that allowed remote audio and video access. Put them on a separate network segment from your primary computers and phones. Change default passwords immediately.

The question of whether intelligence gathering on foreign targets is espionage or national security is genuinely contested. The U.S. conducts extensive cyber operations against foreign governments. Every major nation does. We are in an ongoing conflict that is never declared and rarely described accurately in public.

Most people are not targets of sophisticated intelligence operations. If you're a civilian with no access to classified information, no work in sensitive industries, and no high-profile political role, the nation-state threat model doesn't apply to you specifically. Basic security hygiene protects against the vast majority of threats you'll actually face. Be appropriately informed, not paralyzed.

Chapter 25: Digital Penance - Recognizing the Damage

The first step in healing is acknowledging the wound. We've spent decades building a digital civilization without understanding the human costs, and now we need to face the truth about what we've done to ourselves and our society.

Stop pretending technology habits are harmless or necessary. The average person checks their phone 96 times per day and spends over seven hours staring at screens. That's not progress. That's compulsion with a charger.

We've traded deep relationships for shallow connections. Families sit together in restaurants staring at separate screens instead of talking to each other. Children learn to compete with devices for their parents' attention. Romantic partners choose social media over intimacy. We're more connected than ever and lonelier than we've ever been.

Our minds have been rewired for distraction and instant gratification. We lost the ability to read books, watch movies, or have conversations without constantly checking for digital stimulation. Attention spans collapsed under the weight of infinite content designed to fragment focus.

Critical thinking eroded as we outsourced judgment to algorithms that feed us information confirming what we already believe. We stopped evaluating sources, weighing evidence, and forming independent opinions. The skills that make democracy possible atrophied from disuse.

Physical health deteriorated as we chose sedentary digital entertainment over active recreation. Exercise became another thing to track and share rather than natural movement. Sleep disruption from blue light exposure and late-night scrolling became epidemic.

Professional competence declined as we relied on digital tools to perform tasks we no longer understood. Navigation, calculation, memory, and communication got outsourced to devices, making us more dependent and less capable.

The societal damage compounds across millions of people making similar choices. Democratic participation decreased as political discourse moved to platforms designed to amplify extreme voices. Civic engagement became sharing angry posts rather than community involvement.

Cultural creativity stagnated as algorithms promoted content similar to existing popular material rather than rewarding genuine innovation. Artists optimized for platform engagement rather than artistic vision. Culture became increasingly homogeneous and formulaic.

Educational outcomes suffered as students struggled to focus on sustained learning when their brains expected constant digital stimulation. Reading comprehension declined. Mathematical reasoning weakened. Historical knowledge fragmented into Wikipedia summaries.

Economic inequality increased as technology concentrated wealth among platform owners while eliminating middle-class jobs through automation. The gig economy created the illusion of entrepreneurship while providing corporate profits without worker protections.

Community bonds dissolved as local involvement gave way to global digital participation that provided the feeling of connection without the responsibilities and rewards of actual membership. We know more about strangers online than our own neighbors.

But recognizing damage isn't cause for despair — it's the foundation for recovery. You can't solve problems you won't acknowledge. Knowing how digital technology exploited human psychology helps you make different choices going forward.

The honest assessment starts with your relationship with technology — how it affects your focus, your relationships, your sleep, your sense of self. Not rejecting technology entirely. Using it consciously rather than being used by it.

Chapter 26: Digital Virtue - Building Better Online Habits

Digital virtue isn't mindfulness. It isn't conscious consumption. It isn't setting an intention before you open TikTok. It is the unglamorous work of rebuilding cognitive and behavioral habits that the internet industry spent billions of dollars dismantling. It is harder than any inspirational framing suggests and simpler than any complicated system requires.

The virtue starts with honesty about the current state. Not 'I use my phone too much' — the specific number. Four hours. Six hours. The apps, the exact counts, the sessions at 2 AM that you don't really remember starting. Look at the data. Your phone has it. The discomfort of seeing those numbers clearly is the beginning of anything real.

Digital virtue is fundamentally about who controls your attention. Every app, algorithm, and notification system on your phone was built by teams of behavioral engineers whose professional goal is to control your attention on behalf of their employer. You are in a contest. Most people don't know they're losing.

Reclaim your mornings first. The first hour of the day sets your cognitive frame for everything that follows. The platform that gets your first attention of the day gets your most receptive, least defended version. That's valuable real estate. Stop giving it away. Charge your phone in the kitchen. Buy an alarm clock. Own your first hour.

Rebuild your ability to focus on one thing. This is a specific, measurable skill that deteriorates with smartphone use and improves with practice. Start with 25-minute blocks of single-task focus with the phone face down in another room. This is uncomfortable initially because your brain has been retrained to expect interruption every few minutes. The discomfort is withdrawal. It passes.

Choose your information environment the way you choose your physical environment. You wouldn't fill your house with things that make you anxious, stupid, and angry. Your digital environment does exactly that if you let the default settings stand. Curate aggressively. Every source, account, and feed that doesn't make you smarter, calmer, or more connected to things that actually matter — cut it.

Invest in relationships that don't require a screen. The social atrophy that comes from replacing in-person relationships with digital ones is real and accelerating. Schedule time with people in person the same way you schedule meetings. Treat cancellations with the same seriousness. Show up.

Create things rather than consuming them. Writing, building, cooking, playing music, making objects — any form of creation changes your relationship to digital consumption because creation is active and consumption is passive. An hour spent making something is qualitatively different from an hour spent scrolling, regardless of what you scroll.

Protect your boredom. This sounds paradoxical and it's the most important thing on this list. Boredom is the cognitive state where your brain resets, consolidates, generates connections, and does the slow background work that produces creativity and clarity. The smartphone industry eliminated boredom as a business strategy. Taking it back is an act of cognitive self-defense.

Digital virtue is not about rejecting technology. The internet is the most powerful tool for human communication, learning, and coordination ever built. Many of the people who designed these platforms and optimized these engagement mechanics pulled their own children out of the systems they built. That's not an argument for abstinence. It's an argument for being the kind of person who uses tools instead of being used by them.

The difference between using the internet and being used by the internet is conscious intention applied consistently over time. You decide what you're there for before you open the app. You stop when you've accomplished it. You don't let the algorithm decide what happens next. You don't scroll because you're bored. You don't check because you're anxious. You use it because you chose to, for a reason you can state.

None of this is easy. If it were easy, it wouldn't require virtue. The word virtue implies difficulty, practice, and failure followed by returning to practice. You will pick up your phone when you didn't mean to. You will fall into scroll sessions you didn't intend. You will spend an evening on something you'll regret spending it on. That's not failure. That's the ongoing condition of being human in an environment engineered against your interests.

What you're building toward is a relationship with technology that serves your actual life — your relationships, your work, your health, your growth — rather than serving the quarterly earnings of companies that have never met you. That relationship is possible. It requires treating it as the ongoing project it is, not the one-time decision it isn't.

The internet promised to make us more human. It's on us to make that actually happen.

Chapter 27: Systemic Solutions - Fixing the Machine

The platforms are not going to fix themselves. They proved that. The decade of 'we're working on it' while internal researchers documented the harm, while teen depression spiked, while elections got manipulated, while the engagement algorithms ran unchanged — that decade is the answer. Corporate self-regulation in the face of profitable exploitation is not a strategy. It's theater.

The legal foundation that enabled all of this is Section 230 of the Communications Decency Act, written in 1996 when the internet was a novelty. It gave platforms immunity from liability for what users post. Reasonable at the time. The problem is that modern platforms don't just host content — they actively amplify it through recommendation algorithms. When Facebook's algorithm chooses to show you something, Facebook made a choice. They should own the consequences of that choice. Section 230 as written says they don't have to. That needs to change.

Antitrust enforcement is the other lever nobody wants to pull. Google controls 92% of global search. Meta owns Facebook, Instagram, and WhatsApp. Amazon dominates both e-commerce and cloud computing. Apple and Google together control the operating systems that every app must run through. This is not a market. It's a series of monopolies collecting rents on human communication and commerce. The same antitrust principles that broke up Standard Oil and AT&T apply here. The political will to apply them is what's missing.

Algorithmic transparency is the minimum requirement for accountability. When a recommendation engine controls what two billion people see about elections, health, and each other, that algorithm is a public system with public consequences. It should be subject to independent auditing — not voluntary transparency reports written by the company's own lawyers, but real third-party access with real teeth. The EU's Digital Services Act took a step in this direction. The U.S. has not.

The deliberate addiction of children deserves its own category of response. App developers currently face no legal liability for intentionally designing products to create compulsive use in minors. The variable reward schedules, infinite scrolls, and notification systems targeting children's developing brains are legal. The tobacco industry was eventually forced to stop advertising to children and disclose health risks. It took decades of litigation and legislation. The tech industry is running the same playbook and needs the same response.

Data ownership is a property rights issue, not a privacy issue. Your behavioral data — where you click, how long you pause, what triggers your anxiety — is being harvested and sold to people you've never met to be used against you in ways you can't see. This should require your ongoing informed consent. The EU's GDPR established the basic principle. Every country without equivalent legislation is allowing its citizens to be strip-mined for data with no recourse.

If you want to do something concrete: vote for politicians who can describe specifically what they intend to do about platform liability, antitrust enforcement, and algorithmic accountability. Not politicians who say 'big tech is bad' — politicians who can tell you what legislation they support and why. These are not marginal technical issues. They determine who controls public discourse in your country, which is to say they determine a great deal about what you're allowed to think.

Support the journalists covering tech accountability. The Markup, Wired, ProPublica, and a small number of others do systematic investigative work on how these systems actually operate. They are the accountability mechanism that currently exists for a sector that mostly governs itself. They need readers and they need funding. Subscription journalism about tech accountability is one of the more direct investments you can make.

Talk to your employer about device policies in meetings. Fight for non-digital alternatives at banks, government offices, and medical practices that are eliminating them. Show up to school board meetings when curriculum about digital literacy is on the agenda. Attend city council meetings when public WiFi infrastructure is being discussed. These are the unglamorous, visible places where the digital future actually gets built.

The tech companies will keep doing what they're doing until the cost of doing it exceeds the benefit. That cost comes from regulation, litigation, and competition — three things that require sustained public pressure on institutions with the power to impose them. Individual choices matter. They are not sufficient. The platforms are systems problems and systems require systemic solutions. Get politically specific about it.

Conclusion: Reclaiming Your Humanity

We built tools to enhance human capability and ended up diminishing human capacity. The digital revolution that promised to make us smarter, more connected, and more free instead made us distracted, isolated, and dependent.

Every chapter in this book documents a different way that digital technology exploited fundamental human psychology for corporate profit. The platforms didn't become toxic by accident. They were designed to capture and monetize human attention, emotion, and behavior using techniques borrowed from gambling, addiction research, and psychological manipulation.

The internet gave us access to all human knowledge and we used it to become less knowledgeable. Social media promised to connect us with everyone and left us lonelier than ever. Smartphones were supposed to put the world at our fingertips and instead put corporate surveillance in our pockets.

But this isn't inevitable. Technology is not destiny. Every digital platform was designed by humans making conscious choices about how to capture and direct human attention.

Different choices would have produced different outcomes — and different choices can still produce better ones.

The question isn't whether technology is good or evil. The question is whether we will consciously choose how to integrate digital tools into human life or allow corporate algorithms to make those choices for us.

Taking back control requires understanding how digital manipulation works. When you know that social media platforms use variable reward schedules to create addiction, you can recognize when you're being psychologically manipulated. When you understand that recommendation engines show you content designed to generate engagement rather than inform you, you can seek out diverse sources of information.

Individual solutions aren't sufficient for problems that require systemic change. We need legislation that treats social media companies like the media companies they actually are. We need regulations that prevent technology platforms from using addiction psychology to capture children's attention. We need antitrust enforcement that breaks up companies that have gained too much power over human communication and information.

Most importantly, we need to remember what we're fighting for. Digital technology should serve human values like truth, beauty, justice, and genuine connection. When platforms optimize for engagement, profit, and data collection instead of human flourishing, they're not serving us — we're serving them.

The goal isn't to eliminate technology or return to some pre-digital past. The goal is to use digital tools intentionally rather than being used by them. Technology should amplify human intelligence, creativity, and connection rather than replacing them with algorithmic substitutes.

None of this is an abstraction. It's choosing to read a book instead of doomscrolling at midnight. It's putting your phone face down at dinner. It's calling someone instead of texting. It's doing one hard thing all the way through without picking up the device. These are not grand gestures. They are the daily reps that rebuild a brain that can be present in its own life.

It means protecting your attention as carefully as you protect your money, because attention is the currency that digital platforms extract from you in exchange for services that claim to be free but cost you your focus, your time, and often your peace of mind.

The internet is one of the most powerful tools ever built. The people who shaped it into what it is now made conscious choices to make it addictive rather than useful, divisive rather than connective, profitable at the expense of everything else. That's not technology's nature. That's a business decision. Business decisions can be changed.

The choice is still ours, but not for long. Every day we delay taking conscious control of our digital lives, algorithms become more sophisticated and our dependencies deepen. The window for choosing human agency over algorithmic control is narrowing.

But here's what they don't want you to know: you have more power than you think.

Every time you put down your phone to look someone in the eye, you're winning. Every time you read a book instead of scrolling a feed, you're winning. Every time you choose to be bored instead of entertained, you're winning.

Every moment of genuine human connection defeats their business model. Every act of sustained attention breaks their psychological chains. Every choice to be present in your own life is a revolution against a system designed to keep you distracted, divided, and dependent.

They need you to believe you're powerless. They need you to think the system is too big to fight. They need you to accept that this is just how things are now.

They're lying.

You are not a user to be exploited. You are not content to be monetized. You are not data to be harvested.

You are a human being with agency, dignity, and the right to live fully in your own life.

The machines are not in control. The algorithms are not inevitable. The platforms are not unstoppable.

Turn off the notifications. Delete the apps. Look up from the screen.

Your humanity is not a product to be sold.

Your attention is not a resource to be mined.

Your life is not content to be consumed.

Take it back.

That's the whole game. Be harder to use than to ignore. Be harder to manipulate than to exploit. Be more present in your actual life than in the performance of it. The platforms are counting on you not to bother. Prove them wrong.

Glossary

Algorithm — The invisible hand deciding what you see, think about, and get angry at. On social media platforms, algorithms don't just sort content — they engineer emotional states, amplify the most provocative material, and route you toward whatever keeps you on the platform longest. The algorithm isn't neutral. It has a job, and that job isn't serving you.

Algorithmic Bias — When a system built on human data produces human prejudice and calls it math. Hiring algorithms reject resumes from certain zip codes. Lending algorithms charge higher rates to certain neighborhoods. Predictive policing software sends more cops to already over-policed areas. The bias doesn't disappear when you remove the human decision-maker. It gets laundered through code and becomes harder to challenge.

Astroturfing — Fake grassroots. The name comes from artificial turf, which looks like something natural but isn't. In practice: a corporation, political party, or foreign government pays firms to generate hundreds of social media accounts, comment threads, and review posts that look like spontaneous public opinion. The goal is to make a manufactured position look like a popular movement. It works well enough that people do it constantly.

Avatar — Your digital stand-in, ranging from a cartoon character in a video game to a photorealistic rendering of yourself in a virtual meeting room. The gap between your avatar and your actual body is where identity experimentation happens — which can be useful, or can become a way to avoid dealing with who you actually are. The metaverse sold avatars as liberation. What they mostly delivered was a more convenient way to be someone else.

Catfishing — Building a fake online identity to deceive someone, most often for emotional or financial manipulation. The catfisher constructs a persona using stolen photos and an invented life story, cultivates genuine emotional investment from the target over weeks or months, then either extracts money or simply disappears. The term comes from a 2010 documentary. The practice is significantly older and nowhere near as romantic as the name suggests.

Clickbait — A headline engineered to make you click before you can think. The formula is reliable: create curiosity, imply something shocking, promise a payoff the article rarely delivers. Clickbait exists because online advertising pays per pageview, which means every click is revenue regardless of what happens after. The content is secondary. Getting you to tap the screen is the whole product.

Children's Online Privacy Protection Act (COPPA) — A 1998 US law designed to protect children under thirteen from having their data collected without parental consent. By the standards of what the internet became, it's a screen door on a submarine. Platforms comply by requiring users to enter a birthdate, which children falsify without consequence. The law doesn't apply at all to teenagers, who represent the majority of the documented harm. It was written when the biggest concern was kids seeing banner ads.

Cloud Storage — Keeping your files on someone else's servers and trusting that they'll still be there, accessible, and private tomorrow. Usually they are. Sometimes they aren't — companies get acquired, services shut down, pricing changes, or data gets breached. The convenience is real. So is the dependency. When you store everything in the cloud, you don't own your files so much as rent access to them from whoever controls the servers.

Cryptocurrency — Digital currency secured by cryptography, existing on decentralized networks rather than through banks or governments. The pitch was financial freedom from institutional control. The reality included spectacular fraud, billions in losses from exchange collapses, ransomware operations funded entirely in crypto, and enough energy consumption to power small countries. Some legitimate uses exist. They are dramatically outnumbered by the scams.

Cyberbullying — Harassment conducted through digital platforms, which transforms ordinary cruelty in two ways: it follows the victim home, and it scales. A schoolyard bully reaches one person. A coordinated online harassment campaign can reach someone at every hour of every day across every platform they use, loop in thousands of strangers who've never met the target, and leave a permanent record. The platforms profit from the engagement it generates.

Cybercrime — Criminal activity conducted over digital networks. The category is enormous: identity theft, financial fraud, romance scams, ransomware, phishing, data breaches, counterfeit goods, illegal marketplaces, and more. What distinguishes cybercrime from traditional crime isn't the harm — it's the scale, the geography, and the asymmetry. One person can rob thousands simultaneously from a country with no extradition treaty. The victims feel it personally. The criminals often don't.

Cyberterrorism — Using digital attacks to cause the kind of fear, disruption, and harm that terrorism has traditionally required bombs and bodies to produce. Shutting down a hospital network, poisoning a water treatment system, or taking down the power grid can injure and kill people without anyone setting foot near the target. The bar to entry is lower than conventional terrorism. The potential damage is comparable.

Cyberwarfare — Nations attacking each other's infrastructure, intelligence networks, elections, and economies through digital means instead of, or alongside, conventional military force. It's ongoing, largely invisible, and rarely declared. The attacks attributed to Russia, China, Iran, and North Korea on Western institutions represent documented history, not speculation. Most of it never becomes public. The war you're not reading about is the one being fought right now.

Data Mining — Analyzing large datasets to find patterns, correlations, and behaviors that aren't obvious at smaller scales. When applied to personal information, it can predict what you'll buy, how you'll vote, when you're likely to be emotionally vulnerable, and what kind of content will keep you engaged. The mining is continuous and largely invisible. You're the ore.

Deepfake — AI-generated media in which someone's face, voice, or likeness has been convincingly replaced with a fabricated version. The technology can put words in anyone's mouth, place them in scenes they never inhabited, and do it well enough to fool people who are trying to detect the fake. Originally notorious for non-consensual pornography. Now used for political disinformation, fraud, and harassment. The cost to produce a convincing deepfake has dropped to nearly zero.

Digital Divide — The gap between people who have reliable access to the internet and the devices to use it, and people who don't. It sounds like a technology problem. It's an access problem, which is to say an economic and political problem. As more essential services — healthcare, government benefits, employment applications, education — move online, being on the wrong side of the divide doesn't just mean missing out on convenience. It means being cut off from basic participation in modern society.

Doxxing — Publishing someone's private information online — home address, workplace, phone number, family members — without their consent and usually with hostile intent. The purpose is to weaponize the crowd: once the information is public, anyone can use it, and the doxxer maintains plausible distance from what happens next. Real-world harassment, stalking, and violence have followed doxxing campaigns often enough that it has been criminalized in many jurisdictions.

Echo Chamber — A media environment where everything you encounter confirms what you already believe. Algorithmic curation is what creates most digital echo chambers: the system learns what you engage with and shows you more of it, gradually filtering out friction and contradiction until your feed is a mirror. The result is not just misinformation. It's a distorted sense of how many people share your views and how reasonable the opposition actually is.

Engagement — What platforms measure instead of value. A like, a share, a comment, a minute spent watching — all engagement, regardless of whether it reflects joy, fury, grief, or compulsion. Because engagement drives advertising revenue, platforms optimize for maximum engagement over all other considerations. The content that generates the most engagement turns out to be outrage, conflict, and anxiety. This is not a coincidence.

Filter Bubble — The personalized information environment created when algorithms show you only what you're likely to agree with, click on, or consume. Eli Pariser coined the term in 2011. The problem has gotten substantially worse since. You and someone with different browsing history, political views, and social connections can use the same platform and inhabit completely different realities — same app, different world.

Gamification — Applying the psychological mechanics of games to things that aren't games. Points, levels, badges, streaks, leaderboards — imported into fitness apps, learning platforms, workplace software, and social media to drive behavior through the same reward loops that make games addictive. When it works as advertised, it motivates. When it's exploitative, it turns basic human activities into Skinner boxes.

Gig Economy — A labor model in which workers are classified as independent contractors and hired through apps rather than as employees. The pitch to workers was flexibility. The reality was flexibility without benefits, wages without floors, and all the risk of self-employment with none of the autonomy. The companies that built the gig economy captured enormous value while systematically avoiding the obligations that employment law was designed to impose.

Hacktivism — Hacking as political protest. The targets vary — authoritarian governments, corporations behaving badly, law enforcement databases, financial systems that activists oppose — but the method is the same: unauthorized access used to expose, disrupt, or embarrass rather than to steal. The moral questions are the same ones that apply to vigilante justice everywhere: who decides what target deserves it, and what happens when someone else uses the same logic with different politics.

Influencer — Someone who has accumulated a large following on social media and uses that audience to promote products, ideas, or a curated version of their own life in exchange for payment. The business model depends on the audience believing the influencer genuinely endorses what they're selling. Most don't. The disclosure requirements exist. The enforcement is weak enough that many influencers ignore them without consequence.

Internet of Things (IoT) — The expanding network of everyday objects — thermostats, refrigerators, doorbells, cars, medical devices — that are connected to the internet and collect data. The convenience is real. The security is usually an afterthought: many IoT devices ship with default passwords, receive no software updates, and provide persistent access to your home and habits to manufacturers, data brokers, and whoever manages to compromise them.

Link Rot — The slow disintegration of the web's connective tissue. URLs break when websites restructure, servers shut down, or companies go out of business. Academic citations, news articles, government documents, and the footnotes of a trillion online arguments point to pages that no longer exist. The internet promised to preserve information permanently. It has instead created a record that decays faster than paper.

Metadata — The data about your data. Not the content of your calls, but who you called, when, how long, and from where. Not the text of your emails, but who sent them to whom and when. Metadata is what the NSA collects in bulk and what the intelligence community insists isn't really surveillance. Your metadata reveals your doctor, your lawyer, your romantic relationships, your political associations, and your daily movements. The claim that it isn't personal is false.

Metaverse — The tech industry's recurring vision of a persistent virtual world where people work, socialize, and spend money through digital avatars instead of in physical reality. The concept has been promised for thirty years and has consistently underdelivered. The most recent iteration cost Meta over thirty billion dollars to build and attracted a population roughly equivalent to a small town. What the metaverse actually delivered was a new venue for harassment and a new asset class for speculation.

Microtransaction — A small in-app purchase, typically for a virtual item, a gameplay advantage, or the removal of artificial friction the developer added specifically to sell its removal. Individually, the amounts feel trivial. Collectively, they represent billions in revenue extracted from players — disproportionately from a small number of heavy spenders, some of whom have the same relationship with microtransactions that compulsive gamblers have with slot machines.

Notification — A message sent by an app to interrupt whatever you're doing and pull you back to the platform. The psychological engineering behind notifications is deliberate: variable timing, red badges that trigger mild anxiety until cleared, and urgency framing that makes every alert feel like something you can't afford to miss. You can turn them off. Most people don't, which is what the apps are counting on.

Paywall — A gate requiring payment before you can read, watch, or access content. Paywalls exist because the advertising model that sustained online media destroyed it at the same time — chasing clicks rather than quality, until quality publication became financially impossible without subscriptions. The paywall is a partial correction. It also concentrates quality information among people who can afford it, which is its own problem.

Phishing — Fraud that works by impersonation. An email that looks like it's from your bank, your employer, or a shipping carrier asks you to click a link and log in. The page looks real. The credentials go to the attacker. Modern phishing is personalized — spear phishing targets specific people using information scraped from their social media and professional profiles. The tell is almost always urgency. Slow down, and most phishing attempts become obvious.

Platform — A digital service that hosts interaction between users and calls itself neutral while actively shaping what those users see, say, and believe. The platform framing matters legally: Section 230 of the Communications Decency Act protects platforms from liability for user content on the theory that they're passive hosts rather than publishers. This distinction made sense in 1996. It doesn't describe what Facebook or YouTube actually are.

Privacy Paradox — The observed gap between what people say they want regarding their privacy and what they actually do. People report caring about privacy in surveys, then hand over their location, browsing history, and biometric data for the convenience of a free app. The paradox is partly genuine ambivalence and partly the result of systems designed to make surrender easier than protection.

Ransomware — Malware that encrypts the victim's files and demands payment — usually in cryptocurrency — for the decryption key. The targets have expanded from private citizens to hospitals, schools, municipal governments, and critical infrastructure. Paying the ransom doesn't guarantee you get your files back. Not paying means losing them. The business model is straightforward extortion, and it generates hundreds of millions of dollars annually.

Recommendation Algorithm — The system that decides what you see next. YouTube's next video. Netflix's next show. TikTok's next clip. The recommendation algorithm's goal is not to show you what's best, most accurate, or most enriching — it's to show you whatever keeps you watching. That turns out to be content that provokes strong emotional responses, which explains a lot about where people who start watching mainstream videos end up six months later.

Surveillance Capitalism — Shoshana Zuboff's term for the economic model in which human experience is claimed as raw material, converted into behavioral data, and sold as predictions about future behavior to advertisers and others who want to influence it. The user isn't the customer. The user's attention, habits, and psychological profile are the product. The services are free because you're paying with something more valuable than money.

Swatting — Calling in a false emergency — a hostage situation, a bomb threat, an active shooter — to send a SWAT team to someone's home as a form of harassment. It started in gaming culture as retaliation in competitive disputes. It spread. People have died during swatting calls when police encountered residents who had no idea what was happening. The perpetrators are almost never in the same city as the target.

Viral Content — Media that spreads rapidly across platforms through sharing, often with little regard for its accuracy or social value. The virality is mechanical: content that provokes a strong emotional reaction gets shared more than content that informs or challenges. Which means the content that spreads fastest is usually the content that confirms what people already believe, outrages them, or tells them something they want to be true. Accuracy is not a factor in the spread.

Zero-Day Exploit — An attack that uses a software vulnerability that nobody has publicly discovered yet — not the vendor, not the security community, not the public. Zero days are valuable because there's no patch to apply and no defense to raise. Intelligence agencies stockpile them. Criminal organizations buy and sell them. When a zero-day is used in an attack, it's often disclosed afterward — which is how we know they exist, and how we know they're being used constantly.

Books by Richard Lowe

See books by Richard Lowe at
https://masterofworlds.com

Get free publishing insights and industry updates at
https://thewritingking.substack.com

For ghostwriting and book coaching services see
https://thewritingking.com

www.ingramcontent.com/pod-product-compliance
Lightning Source LLC
Chambersburg PA
CBHW030932060726
47591CB00005B/1764